D1443013

Angelina Jolie

Other books in the People in the News series:

Angelina Jolie

By Bonnie Szumski and Jill Karson

LUCENT BOOKS
A part of Gale, Cengage Learning

GALE
CENGAGE Learning·

Detroit • New York • San Francisco • New Haven, Conn • Waterville, Maine • London

Library of Congress Cataloging-in-Publication Data

Szumski, Bonnie, 1958-
   Angelina Jolie / by Bonnie Szumski and Jill Karson.
   pages cm. -- (People in the news)
   Includes bibliographical references and index.
   ISBN 978-1-4205-0750-8 (hardcover)
1. Jolie, Angelina, 1975---Biography--Juvenile literature. 2. Motion
picture actors and actresses--United States--Biography--Juvenile
literature. I. Karson, Jill. II. Title.
   PN2287.J583S97 2013
   791.4302'8092--dc23
   [B]
                                                          2013028046

Lucent Books
27500 Drake Rd
Farmington Hills MI 48331

ISBN-13: 978-1-4205-0750-8
ISBN-10: 1-4205-0750-8

Printed in the United States of America
1 2 3 4 5 6 7 17 16 15 14 13

Contents

Fame and celebrity are alluring. People are drawn to those who walk in fame's spotlight, whether they are known for great accomplishments or for notorious deeds. The lives of the famous pique public interest and attract attention, perhaps because their experiences seem in some ways so different from, yet in other ways so similar to, our own.

Newspapers, magazines, and television regularly capitalize on this fascination with celebrity by running profiles of famous people. For example, television programs such as *Entertainment Tonight* devote all their programming to stories about entertainment and entertainers. Magazines such as *People* fill their pages with stories of the private lives of famous people. Even newspapers, newsmagazines, and television news frequently delve into the lives of well-known personalities. Despite the number of articles and programs, few provide more than a superficial glimpse at their subjects.

Lucent's People in the News series offers young readers a deeper look into the lives of today's newsmakers, the influences that have shaped them, and the impact they have had in their fields of endeavor and on other people's lives. The subjects of the series hail from many disciplines and walks of life. They include authors, musicians, athletes, political leaders, entertainers, entrepreneurs, and others who have made a mark on modern life and who, in many cases, will continue to do so for years to come.

These biographies are more than factual chronicles. Each book emphasizes the contributions, accomplishments, or deeds that have brought fame or notoriety to the individual and shows how that person has influenced modern life. Authors portray their subjects in a realistic, unsentimental light. For example, Bill Gates—cofounder of the software giant Microsoft—has been instrumental in making personal computers the most vital tool of the modern age. Few dispute his business savvy, his perseverance, or his technical expertise, yet critics say he is ruthless in his dealings with competitors and driven more by his desire to maintain Microsoft's dominance in the computer industry than by an interest in furthering technology.

In these books, young readers will encounter inspiring stories about real people who achieved success despite enormous obstacles. Oprah Winfrey—one of the most powerful, most watched, and wealthiest women in television history—spent the first six years of her life in the care of her grandparents while her unwed mother sought work and a better life elsewhere. Her adolescence was colored by pregnancy at age fourteen, rape, and sexual abuse.

Each author documents and supports his or her work with an array of primary and secondary source quotations taken from diaries, letters, speeches, and interviews. All quotes are footnoted to show readers exactly how and where biographers derive their information and provide guidance for further research. The quotations enliven the text by giving readers eyewitness views of the life and accomplishments of each person covered in the People in the News series.

In addition, each book in the series includes photographs, annotated bibliographies, timelines, and comprehensive indexes. For both the casual reader and the student researcher, the People in the News series offers insight into the lives of today's newsmakers—people who shape the way we live, work, and play in the modern age.

Committed to Life

A ngelina Jolie is a successful movie actress as well as a human-itarian, who travels around the world bringing attention to refugees, people who have been displaced from their homes due to war or a natural disaster. Her life is both extraordinary and ordinary. She is the daughter of Jon Voight, also a successful actor, and he exposed her to the world of movies and acting at an early age (her first role came at age seven). Jolie also experienced distress at an early age when her parents divorced.

Learning to Love Life

As a young woman, Jolie acted out in extreme ways. Besides taking drugs she was a self-cutter (self-cutters are usually young people between seven and twenty-four years old who cut themselves with a knife or other sharp object to relieve stress). Jolie's self-destructive behavior could have killed her.

Acting drew Jolie out of this dark place. Specifically the role of Gia Carangi in the movie *Gia* (1998). Carangi was a fashion model who died at the age of twenty-six. Like Jolie, Carangi also had parents who divorced when she was young, and she did drugs. But Carangi contracted AIDS (acquired immunodeficiency syndrome) from an infected needle and died from the disease. Jolie said that playing Carangi was key to pulling her out of her own self-destructive behavior.

Jolie then embraced life with a vengeance. She once told an interviewer, "The only thing I am good at, seriously? Is living every single day as fully as possible. Doing every possible thing I

Angelina Jolie has used her celebrity to bring awareness to problems in other parts of the world. Pictured here, Jolie visits a refugee camp in the Democratic Republic of the Congo in March 2013.

can damn well do for the people I love at every moment—make some big decisions quick, spit them out and move on."[1] This statement proved true for the rest of Jolie's life, as she gained inspiration from her various acting roles, her humanitarian efforts, and her role as a mother.

Realizing Her Mission

Part of Jolie's movie, *Lara Croft: Tomb Raider* (2001), was filmed in Angkor, Cambodia, and while Jolie was in the country she witnessed the dire poverty of the people, many of them refugees. The plight of Cambodia's children, many of whom had been maimed by land mines (highly explosive devices that are buried in the ground during war to injure or kill the enemy when he steps or drives over it), especially moved her. She wanted to do something to help them and thus embarked on an ongoing mission of fund-raising, on-the-ground fieldwork, and other acts of generosity that have changed the lives of many of the world's refugees and brought awareness to their situation. In fact, Jolie has pursued humanitarian work with such focus that she is now almost as well-known for her charity efforts as she is for her acting. Even though the people she helps have been through war, crime, rape, and violence, Jolie says that in helping them, she is able to see the best of human nature. "The courage, resilience, and quiet dignity of returnee families rebuilding their lives against the kind of adversity few of us can imagine shows the human spirit at its best,"[2] she said.

Jolie's humanitarian efforts, in turn, inspired her to become a mother, another role for which she is famous. She adopted her first child, Maddox, from Cambodia in 2002. A decade later, in 2012, she had three biological children and three adopted children. In her role as mother, she found her most important and fulfilling purpose. "I want to raise children who will be good people and be a positive influence in this world," she says, adding that beyond acting, directing, writing, or doing humanitarian work, "I would say being a mother comes first."[3]

Jolie continues to impress people with her willingness to live life to its fullest and drive herself to be her best. She firmly believes that people make their own lives and does not let her rocky start in life dictate the person she is today. "Life is very much about family and the family you choose," she explains. "You can define your own destiny despite what happened to you in the past."[4]

Chapter 1

A Life Apart

Like many children of famous people, Angelina Jolie received attention just for being the daughter of a movie star. While her physical beauty and famous father allowed her to establish a career early in life, they also brought her a great deal of sadness and pain. Unshielded from her parents' divorce and with little guidance from her parents, she turned her early sadness into self-destructive behavior that led her into darkness and depression.

Divorced Parents

Angelina Jolie Voight was born on June 4, 1975, in Los Angeles, California, to actor Jon Voight and actress Marcheline Bertrand. Jolie was the couple's second child. Their first, James Haven, was born in 1973. Bertrand quit acting after her son was born to devote herself to parenting her children. Unfortunately, Voight and Bertrand could not keep their marriage together, and they separated in 1976, when Jolie was six months old. Bertrand filed for divorce in 1978, and it became final in 1980. Bertrand promptly began a relationship with documentary filmmaker Bill Day. Although the couple never married, they lived together for eleven years.

Voight and Bertrand divorced at the peak of Voight's career; in 1979 he won an Academy Award for the movie *Coming Home* (1978). Voight left Bertrand for another actress, a move he would later regret. "The break-up of my marriage left emotional scars on my kids,"[5] he once said. During this period, Voight experienced a crisis in both his personal and professional lives. "I guess you

Angelina's parents, Marcheline Bertrand and Jon Voight, pictured in 1972, separated when she was just six months old.

could say I was lost," he said. "I was in a retreat from a success that I didn't understand and wasn't comfortable with."[6]

Jolie was greatly affected by the divorce of her parents, and she was often unhappy. She once told a reporter that she remembered looking at the sky from her crib. "I've just been staring out a window all my life, thinking there was somewhere I could finally be grounded and happy. I belonged somewhere else."[7]

Initially Voight remained close to his children, and Jolie relished being daddy's little girl. Voight remembers, "I sat Angie down and asked her what kind of girl she thought her father should be with. She thought about it for a while and then said, 'Well, Daddy, maybe me, because I love you more than anything in the world.'"[8] Voight, however, had a hard time being consistent with his attention. He later admitted that he struggled with his role as a father, never quite seeing how he fit into his daughter's life. Jolie says he was "the perfect example of an artist who couldn't be married. He had the perfect family but there's something about it that's very scary for him."[9]

Saying the smoggy Los Angeles air was bad for her health, Bertrand moved with the children and Day to Palisades, New York, a small town 25 miles (40km) north of New York City. There, they lived in an apartment, and Jolie remembers wanting a house with "an attic of things that I could go back up and look at."[10]

A Budding Actress

Even though Jolie often felt isolated as a child, she was definitely a budding actress from an early age. As a young girl, she liked to play dress up, wearing plastic high-heeled shoes, frilly clothing, and sparkly decorations. Her brother was the videographer at her impromptu performances. He loved to aim a video camera at her and ask her to perform.

Jolie would act out skits and jokes to make people laugh. Her brother recalls Jolie pretending to perform in a commercial for Subway sandwiches, in which she said, "I'll punch your face if you don't buy a sandwich."[11] Jolie's love of acting was fueled by her mother's love of movies, and they often went to the movies together. One of Jolie's early favorites was the Disney movie *Dumbo* (1941).

When Jolie was four years old, her father's movie, *The Champ* (1979), came out. In it Voight plays a boxer who dies from boxing injuries. When Jolie and her brother watched the movie, both

As children Angelina, seen here at age 4, and her brother James lived for a time in New York with their mother, but saw their father on occasion.

grew distressed and worried that their father had really died. Voight recalls, "They both started weeping. The last scene was very unsettling. I had to take them in my arms and explain that Daddy was just acting—that he wasn't dead, that he was still here with them."[12]

When Jolie was seven years old, Voight got her a small part in his movie, *Lookin' to Get Out* (1982). Voight plays a

Jon Voight

Jon Voight, Angelina Jolie's father, was born December 29, 1938, in Yonkers, New York. His acting career took shape in the 1960s when he appeared on various television shows, including several episodes of the popular, prime-time Western *Gunsmoke*. Soon after, he drew positive praise for his theatrical performance as Rodolfo in the play *A View from the Bridge* and for his movie debut in *Fearless Frank* (1967). Voight then landed the role that would make him an overnight star: Joe Buck, a country boy from Texas who becomes a male hustler in New York City in the movie *Midnight Cowboy* (1969). With its sordid themes and bold content, *Midnight Cowboy* received an X rating and remains notable as the only X-rated film to win the Academy Award for best picture.

Voight also received critical acclaim for his performance in the movie *Deliverance* (1972), in which he plays a businessman who goes on an ill-fated canoe trip. Other prominent roles include a paraplegic Vietnam veteran in *Coming Home* (1978), for which he won the Academy Award for best actor, and a penniless ex-boxing champion in *The Champ* (1979). Voight also appears as Mr. Sir in the comedy-fantasy *Holes* (2003); as Patrick Gates in the action-adventure *National Treasure* (2004) and its sequel, *National Treasure: Book of Secrets* (2007); and as U.S. secretary of defense John Keller in the blockbuster *Transformers* (2007). As of early 2013, Voight had appeared in more than sixty movies and other productions.

wayward gambler, and Jolie plays the daughter of the gambler's ex-girlfriend. Although the movie received poor reviews and remains largely forgotten, many die-hard Jolie fans have nonetheless watched the movie, as it marks her screen debut.

Unafraid of Death

Jolie started elementary school in New York at a public school. She had friends at school, and she became part of a group known as the Kissy Girls that chased boys, held them down, and kissed and bit them until they screamed. Teachers quickly put an end to the game and reprimanded Jolie.

In 1985 Jolie's grandfather (her mother's father, Rolland Bertrand) died from cancer. Jolie was nine years old. She was very upset with his funeral; she thought that there should have been more celebration about his life. She began to wear black, started reading about embalming and mortuary science, and took visits to graveyards. In an interview years later she admitted she even completed a degree by mail to be a funeral director. "I'm not scared of death, which makes people think I'm dark, when in fact I'm positive," she once said. "The thought that you could die tomorrow frees you to appreciate life now."[13]

Tough Times

When Jolie was eleven years old, she and her family moved back to California, settling in the Los Angeles area. Although Voight was relatively wealthy, the star did not share his wealth with his children and often failed to even pay the child support he was required to pay to their mother. Bertrand struggled to support her children, who had to wear secondhand clothes. Many students at school made fun of her clothes. They also teased her about her braces, glasses, full lips, and skinny body. Jolie remembers this time as the beginning of when she started feeling sad and disconnected. She recalls that her life "started not to be fun."[14] Because of her problems at school, issues with

In her preteen years Angelina would attend fancy Hollywood events with her actor father, while at the same time her mother was struggling financially to take care of Angelina and her brother.

self-esteem, and her mother's struggles with money, Jolie and her mother shared what Jolie called an "us against the world"[15] mentality.

Jolie's relationship with her father was decidedly different. It was strained, and they often argued. Jolie and her brother, James, also think that Voight did not treat their mother very well. In a 2007 interview James explained,

> I have horrible memories of my father and the way he behaved. He was so tough on our mother. . . . He lived in the same town. We saw him around Christmas time or at school recitals. He was always around but he never did his job as a father. I think one of the reasons Angelina and I care so much for other people is his treatment of our mother. Angelina and I were very protective of her for that reason.[16]

Developing an Acting Identity

As a teenager, Jolie remained interested in acting. In 1986 she dropped out of high school and enrolled at the Lee Strasberg Theatre and Film Institute in West Hollywood, California. The institute was an acting academy established in 1969 by Lee Strasberg, a famous actor and director. Strasberg taught actors a technique known as method acting, whereby actors try to feel the emotions of their characters by calling on their own painful or otherwise emotionally profound memories. Jolie studied at the institute for two years but left because she decided she was too young to have sufficient memories to help her portray her characters.

She returned to high school, where teasing from other students resumed as before. Jolie began to feel more isolated than ever. She brooded over her sadness and isolation. Referring to these days, she says, "I was always that punk in school. . . . I didn't feel clean [or] pretty."[17] These broodings led to dangerous, self-destructive, and even suicidal thoughts. She started "thinking about not wanting to be around. . . . It was when the reality of life set in, the reality of surviving."[18]

Angelina, pictured here in 1988, attended acting school in her early teens, but returned to high school after two years.

Beautiful Knives

When she was a young girl, Angelina Jolie often accompanied her mother and brother to renaissance fairs, excursions that the young Jolie found fascinating. As a result, she developed a love of weaponry, which is unusual for a young girl. Jolie says,

> I went to the Renaissance Fair with my mom when I was a little girl and there were all these kinda knives . . . . It reminds you of history and there's something really beautiful and traditional about them, and just different countries have different weapons and blades, and there's something beautiful about them to me. So I began collecting knives—I've collected weapons since I was a little girl.

Quoted in Kathleen Tracy. *Angelina Jolie: A Biography.* Westport, CT. Greenwood Press, 2009. www.wosco.org/books/Art/Angelina_Jolie.pdf.

A Wild Child

As Jolie became more rebellious, her outward appearance changed to reflect her inner turmoil and deep sadness. She wore grungy, black-leather clothing and boots and had many piercings. Her school notebooks often featured drawings of knives and comments about death.

Jolie's mother did not place many restrictions on her or provide much guidance. Her new, strange behaviors caused her mother to fear she was losing her daughter's love. Rather than set boundaries for her daughter, Bertrand accommodated her in order to keep her close. Jolie had her first serious boyfriend when she was fourteen, and her mother allowed the two to live together in her daughter's bedroom. Her boyfriend introduced Jolie to drugs, which the two did frequently. The couple also frequented punk music clubs and experimented with sex.

After a while, the two began to self-cut to alleviate their feelings of sadness. Jolie says that she and her boyfriend cut each other as a desperate way of experiencing intimacy. "I started having sex and sex didn't feel like enough and my emotions didn't feel like enough," she remembers. "My emotions kept wanting to break out. In a moment of wanting something honest, I grabbed a knife and cut my boyfriend—and he cut me. . . . It felt so primitive and it felt so honest, but then I had to deal with not telling my mother, hiding things, wearing gauze bandages to school."[19] Even though she hid it from her mother, the cutting continued. Jolie recalls, "For some reason, the ritual of having cut myself and feeling . . . the pain, maybe, feeling alive, feeling some kind of release, it was somehow therapeutic to me."[20]

One day Jolie had to be rushed to the hospital after she cut her neck so badly that she almost cut her jugular vein, which could have been fatal. Following this harrowing event, Jolie broke up with her boyfriend. At the same time, her mother allowed her to move into her own apartment across from hers.

When she was older, Jolie criticized her younger self as being overly dramatic and self-centered. "I think now that if somebody would have taken me at 14 and dropped me in the middle of Asia or Africa, I'd have realized how self-centered I was, and that there was real pain and real death, real things to fight for. I wouldn't have been fighting myself so much," she says. "I wish when I was thinking about suicide, I'd have seen how many people are dying each day that have no choice in the matter. I would have appreciated the fact that I had a choice."[21] But with little experience of a larger world at the time and with little parental influence, Jolie made decisions by herself, and some of these had dire consequences.

Chapter 2

A Turbulent Start

L ike most young women, Angelina Jolie spent her late teens and early twenties finding herself and deciding what she wanted to do with her life. Unlike most young women, however, Jolie became a model at the age of sixteen and an actress at eighteen, working in an industry that was immensely competitive and often critical. As her career progressed, she also had to learn how to deal with media attention, something that even veteran actors often find challenging.

A Model Start

By the age of sixteen, Jolie was a beautiful young woman with exotic features, including the large, pillowy lips that had made her an object of ridicule in high school. Her beauty and voluptuous figure landed her a job at the modeling agency Finesse Model Management. Jolie's modeling assignments took her to Los Angeles, California; New York, New York; and London, England. The job afforded her some financial security, but it never interested her as a career. She stopped modeling at the age of eighteen, saying, "I couldn't take the pressure of always trying to be taller and skinnier and stuff."[22]

Jolie's modeling experience led to her appearance in a few music videos, a booming industry in the early 1990s. Jolie appeared alongside some well-known rock figures, including singer Meat Loaf in the video *Rock 'n' Roll Dreams Come Through* and with the band the Rolling Stones in *Anybody Seen My Baby?* During this period, her brother entered film school at the University of

Jolie's unique beauty earned her a successful modeling career in the early 1990s.

Southern California in Los Angeles, and she performed in a number of his student films. Yet the young actress remained ambivalent about whether acting was right for her. After she graduated from high school, she decided to go back to the Lee Strasberg institute to learn more about acting.

Jolie also turned to her famous father for coaching and advice. Every week the two would get together and act out scenes from plays. As Voight said of this period, "She'd come over to my house and we'd run through a play together, performing various parts. I saw that she had real talent. She loved acting. So I did my best to encourage her, to coach her and to share my best advice with her. For a while, we were doing a new play together every Sunday."[23]

Around this time, Jolie dropped her last name, Voight, and became known only as Angelina Jolie. She said, "I dropped my name because it was important that I was my own person."[24] She did not want to be getting auditions and roles just because she was Jon Voight's daughter. She wanted to achieve her own success.

Jolie's first roles as an adult were in small plays. When she auditioned for a role in the play *Room Service*, which features two main female characters, she actually had her eye on the role of the male hotel owner, Gregory Wagner. Jolie recalls, "I thought, you

Doing It on Her Own

Angelina Jolie's father, Jon Voight, was supportive of his daughter early in her movie career, even when she dropped her last name. In a 1996 interview, Jolie explained,

> When I decided to become an actress, he didn't force me, he knew I wanted to do it on my own. I dropped my name because it was important that I was my own person. . . . But now it's great because we can talk on a level few people can talk to their parents on. Not only can we talk about our work, but our work is about our emotions, our lives, the games we play, what goes through our heads.

Quoted in *Empire*. "Jonny Lee Miller and Angelina Jolie—the Happy Couple," June 1996. http://angelanna3.tripod.com/interviews/id1.html.

know, which character do I want to audition for? The big, fat, 40-year-old German man—that's the part for me."[25] Jolie got the part and played it as a man, even though it was traditionally played by a male actor. When her father saw the play, he exclaimed, "Oh my God, she's just like me. She'll take these crazy parts and be thrilled that she can make people chuckle or whatever."[26]

A Female Cyborg

With her confidence growing, Jolie relocated to New York City and enrolled in night classes at New York University, where she majored in film. Shortly after the move, she landed her first movie role as an adult. It was Cash Reese, a female cyborg, in *Cyborg 2* (1993), a sequel to the 1989 movie *Cyborg*, a futuristic science-fiction thriller. Reese is supposed to seduce her way into a rival manufacturer's workplace and then blow herself up. She fails to complete her mission, however, because she falls in love with a human.

While the first *Cyborg* movie was a hit and launched the career of actor Jean-Claude Van Damme, *Cyborg 2* never made it into movie theaters and went straight to video. Critics who saw the prerelease of the film gave it particularly poor reviews, rocking Jolie's confidence. She later said, "If you have enough people sitting around telling you you're wonderful, then you start believing you're fabulous. Then someone tells you you stink, and you believe that, too."[27]

The poor reviews also left her depressed and experiencing the same suicidal feelings she had when she was younger. Her isolation in New York City also left her feeling down. "I didn't have any close friends anymore and the city just seemed cold and sad and strange," she said. "Everything that was kind of romantic about New York just got very cold for me."[28] She says that seeing a beautiful kimono (a long, loose, Japanese robe) in a shop window pulled her out of her depression. She realized that her desire to wear it would never be fulfilled if she killed herself. She repeatedly looked back on this period of sadness as the one that made her realize she had to live each day as if it were her last, instead of longing for life to be over.

The 1995 movie **Hackers** *is Jolie's first notable acting role after a couple of forgettable initial roles.*

Despite her newfound enthusiasm for life, she still had a difficult time getting roles that would showcase her talents. She got a small part in a 1995 crime-drama movie titled *Without Evidence*, but it also received negative reviews.

Hackers

Jolie's next role was in the 1995 movie *Hackers*, starring Jonny Lee Miller, a twenty-two-year-old British actor. Miller plays Dade Murphy, a teenage computer hacker, and Jolie plays Kate Libby, one of Murphy's classmates. Like Jolie's previous two movies, *Hackers* received mostly poor reviews. Hal Hinson of the *Washington Post* newspaper was one of the reviewers who did not like the movie, even casting aspersions on Jolie's appearance, writing that her "lips are so pouty and bee-stung that they seem about to explode."[29]

Some reviewers, however, liked the movie, including well-known movie critic Roger Ebert, who writes, "Jolie, the daughter of Jon Voight, and Miller, a British newcomer, bring a particular quality to their performances that is convincing and engaging."[30]

Like their characters in the movie, Jolie and Miller became romantically involved during filming. The relationship would be the first for Jolie since her boyfriend in high school.

In Search of a Pivotal Role

Jolie continued to make movies, including the romantic comedy *Mojave Moon* (1996) and a modernized version of the Romeo and Juliet story, *Love Is All There Is* (1996). Neither caught on with a wide audience. Many actresses are picky about choosing roles they feel are worthy of them. Jolie's attitude was different: She once told an interviewer that she needed to take roles just to keep her name in the minds of moviegoers and movie producers.

Although critics did not like the 1996 movie Foxfire, *many recognized Jolie, second from right, as a bright spot in the cast.*

With *Foxfire* (1996), however, Jolie finally gained positive attention for her acting. The movie is based on the book, *Foxfire: Confessions of a Girl Gang*, written by Joyce Carol Oates, in which a group of schoolgirls take revenge on an abusive teacher. Jolie plays Legs Sadovsky, who is the ringleader of the girls. Although critics did not like it, several complimented Jolie for being the most engaging actor in the movie. Melanie Greene, coproducer of one of Jolie's later movies, says that Jolie has "the wisdom of an old soul . . . the grace and style of an older woman. You want to peel away the layers when you meet her."[31]

Murder Better than Suicide

Angelina Jolie has spoken publicly about her bouts of depression that were sometimes so severe that she contemplated suicide. In a 2003 interview, Jolie describes how she once tried to hire someone to kill her so she could spare her family and friends the guilt that is often associated with suicide:

This is going to sound insane, but there was a time I was going to hire somebody to kill me. The person spoke very sweetly to me, he made me think about it for a month. And, after a month, other things changed in my life and I was surviving again. With suicide comes all the guilt of people around you thinking they could have done something. With somebody being murdered, nobody takes some kind of guilty responsibility.

Quoted in Rhona Mercer. *Angelina Jolie: The Biography.* London: John Blake, 2007, p. 53.

The movie is also notable for helping to secure Jolie's reputation as wild and unpredictable. While working on the film, Jolie became romantically involved with a costar, the female model and actor Jenny Shimizu, even though she was still in a relationship with Miller. Jolie states, "I realized that I was looking at [Shimizu] in a way that I had looked at men. And it was great, and it was a discovery. It had never crossed my mind that I was going to one day experiment with or kiss a woman, it was never something I was looking for. I just happened to fall for a girl."[32]

An Unconventional Wedding

Jolie told Miller about her affair with Shimizu, and the couple remained together. In March 1996 they married. Jolie was just twenty years old, and Miller was twenty-three. The wedding was private, with only two guests in attendance. Miller wore leather, while Jolie wore a white shirt and black rubber pants. The shirt had Miller's name on it in Jolie's blood. The couple also got tattoos to mark the event. When asked to explain why she would marry a costar, Jolie said, "Look . . . it's a specific type of personality that goes into this job. As actors, you have a lot in common and you expose yourselves to each other emotionally. You see into each other pretty quickly. And you have down time where you get to know each other, so it's kind of an ideal situation. You get to know each other at a really deep level."[33]

While the couple was in love, their marriage was difficult to sustain. Because of their careers, the young couple was almost never together. When Jolie wanted to relocate from Los Angeles to New York, Miller decided to move back to London. He missed his home and did not want to move to yet a third city. Jolie, however, never felt at home in Miller's London apartment. With the two in separate cities, the marriage quickly fell apart, and they separated after only eighteen months and divorced in 1999.

Jolie's brief marriage to her Hackers co-star Jonny Lee Miller came to an end after eighteen months.

No One Quite Like Angelina

Meanwhile Jolie filmed her next movie, a comedy titled *Playing God* (1997), in which she plays a gangster's girlfriend. During filming, history repeated itself as Jolie briefly became romantically

In the 1997 TV movie George Wallace, Jolie won rave reviews—and her first Golden Globe Award—as Cornelia, seen here, Wallace's Southern wife.

involved with her costar, Timothy Hutton, even though she was still married to Miller. Also the same: Critics disliked the movie.

While Jolie was struggling to find movie roles that would garner respect, she decided to perform on television. She accepted parts in two made-for-television movies. The first, a Western miniseries called *True Women*, was released in 1997. It is about the lives of three women in the 1850s. Jolie plays one of the women. She received positive reviews for her performance, which includes a poignant scene in which she must sing her dying child to sleep.

The second movie, also released in 1997, is a docudrama about former Alabama governor George Wallace. Wallace is known for his support of segregation in the 1960s and for his four unsuccessful campaigns for president of the United States. Jolie plays Cornelia, the governor's second wife. She received positive reviews for her acting and for her Southern accent. She received a Golden Globe Award for her performance. John Frankenheimer, the director of *George Wallace*, said, "The world is full of beautiful girls. But they're not Angelina Jolie. She's fun, honest, intelligent, gorgeous and divinely talented."[34]

Jolie's roles in television established her reputation as a serious actress. She was finally getting attention for her work. Still, Jolie worried about the types of roles available to her. "I seem to be getting a lot of [roles] pushed my way that are strong women, but the wrong type of strong women," she said at the time. "It's like people see *Hackers* and they send me offers to play tough women with guns, the kind who wear no bra and a little tank top. I'd like to play strong women who are also very feminine."[35]

The frantic pace she maintained by making several movies within just a couple of years left her exhausted. Yet Jolie believed that she had to continue to act in order to not be forgotten. She was remarkably practical, a virtue that would benefit her in the years ahead.

Chapter 3

A Successful Actress

While still in her early twenties, Angelina Jolie established an unconventional lifestyle that overshadowed her movie career and led many movie critics to discount her abilities. Yet Jolie eventually became a respected actress by playing a series of powerful roles.

Playing Gia

In 1997 Jolie auditioned for the lead character in *Gia*, a made-for-television movie about lesbian supermodel Gia Carangi, who led a short, intense life filled with drugs and sex. The model died of AIDS in 1986 at the age of twenty-six. Fearing the intensity of the role and the ways in which Carangi's life paralleled her own, Jolie changed her mind about wanting the role and turned the part down four times. She did not want to take on a role that so closely imitated her own pain and struggles. "There was a lot of the story that I really identified with, so I didn't want to touch it," she confessed. "I just didn't want to deal with it. She had a lot of pain. Gia was emotionally and literally raped, but she had such a fire for life and in her love for women. She had these incredible crazy moments, and she was always attacking everything she wanted, just going for it."[36]

In the end, Jolie accepted the part, and it turned out to be a wise choice. The role allowed the actress to show she could play a complex character. Indeed, Jolie and Carangi had several things in common—both were incredibly beautiful, tough, collected knives, and experimented with drugs and unconventional sex.

Playing the role of real-life supermodel Gia Carangi, who died of AIDS in 1986, in the TV movie Gia earned Jolie her second Golden Globe Award.

Unlike Jolie, however, Carangi became addicted to hard drugs and contracted AIDS (acquired immunodeficiency syndrome) by using an infected needle.

As Carangi, Jolie needed to express intense emotions, so she stayed in character even when not on the set. To play Carangi at the end of her life when she was wasting away from her illness, Jolie went as far as to actually shave her head instead of hiding her hair under a bald wig. She also had Kaposi's sarcomas (terrible sores that accompany end-stage AIDS) painted onto her body. Her efforts were worth it. After the movie aired on the HBO cable channel in 1998, Jolie received rave reviews. Michele Greppi writes in the *New York Post* newspaper, "Most of the credit for this [movie] must go to Angelina Jolie. She fearlessly, even recklessly throws herself into every second. Every moment, every silence, every big, globby tear is a dare to everyone around her to keep up. The result is unforgettable."[37] Jolie received her second Golden Globe Award for her unforgettable performance as Gia Carangi.

Yet, Jolie's success in the movie left her feeling empty. The feeling surprised her. She had become so absorbed in the role and identified so deeply with Carangi's self-destructive tendencies, that, when the movie was finished, she felt strangely unmoored. She stated in interviews that she felt she had to find her own identity again. Like other times in her life, Jolie rallied herself. She plunged herself into acting, appearing in five movies in a little over a year.

Better Roles

In Jolie's next movies she continued to have better roles and her performances were well received. In *Playing by Heart* (1998), a romance with a large ensemble cast, Jolie plays Joan, a club-hopping, joke-cracking woman looking for love. The movie never had a wide audience, but movie critics praised Jolie. Roger Ebert writes, "Jolie steals the movie as a woman whose personal style has become so entertaining, she can hide behind it,"[38] while James Berardinelli writes, "Angelina Jolie, who gives the film's standout performance, is luminous."[39]

In *The Bone Collector* (1999), a crime drama, Jolie plays a police investigator who helps hunt for a serial killer. She prepared for the role by interviewing real police investigators and by going to a morgue to view dead bodies. Jolie believed that this research would help her give a realistic performance. While reviewers did not like the movie, audiences did.

Outspoken About Everything

Angelina Jolie has never shied away from controversy. Rather, her willingness early in her career to divulge intimate details about her life made her a favorite target of reporters. In an interview that appeared in a 2000 issue of *Esquire* magazine, Jolie explains how the people in her life, including her father, wished she would not share so much and how the press often twists what she says:

> I'm really outspoken and I think he's [Jon Voight] been worried about me. . . . 'Cause I've talked about, you know, everything. And just being really outspoken about my marriage and, you know, being with women, and they [the press] will take it and turn it into different things. So he's wanting me to kind of be quiet. A lot of people have wanted me to be quiet. A lot of people wanted me to be quiet during [the filming of the 1998 movie] *Gia*, to not say if I'd ever done any drugs...which to me was being totally hypocritical. If I had, and if I could identify with the story that much more, and really saw a beautiful thing in another woman—so I thought it was nice to share what I had experienced, 'cause I thought it was great—I didn't see why it was so bad.

Quoted in John H. Richardson. "Angelina Jolie and the Torture of Fame." *Esquire*, February 1, 2000. www.esquire.com/features/angelina-jolie-torture-fame-0200.

A Pivotal Role

Reviewers were more enthusiastic about Jolie's next movie, *Girl, Interrupted* (1999). A drama based on the book of the same name written by Susanna Kaysen, it is the true story of Kaysen's nearly two-year stay in a mental institution. Actress Winona Ryder plays Kaysen, and Jolie plays a fellow patient named Lisa Rowe, who is a brash psychopath. Jolie wanted the part as soon as she knew the book was going to become a movie. She contacted James Mangold, the movie's director and screenwriter, and expressed her interest. As it turned out, Mangold was already thinking of her for the role of Rowe, and her audition clinched it. Mangold knew that Jolie could play the part. He said, "There was someone speaking through her, it was a part of herself. . . . I not only knew I had Lisa [Rowe], but that I also had confidence in the movie I had written."[40]

Even though Jolie's part was a supporting one, the actress stole every scene she was in. Film critic James Brundage praised Jolie, writing that she "works wonders in her role as a sociopath, giving a performance that makes you absolutely believe in the amorality of her character."[41] Movie producer Douglas Wick compared Jolie's acting talents with those of acclaimed actor Jack Nicholson, who won an Academy Award for his performance as a patient in a mental institution in the movie *One Flew over the Cuckoo's Nest* (1975). "Lisa does terrible things," Wick says. "The amazing thing

In **Girl, Interrupted** *Jolie's powerful performance as a mental institution patient cemented her reputation as a gifted actress while earning her an Academy Award for Best Supporting Actress.*

is that [Jolie] has something that Jack Nicholson has which is that she can do very bad things [as her character] and somehow do them in a way that [makes her character remain] fascinating."[42] Jolie's life again mirrored Nicholson's when she received the Academy Award for best supporting actress for her performance. She also won a Golden Globe Award.

Billy Bob

Jolie's next movie was *Pushing Tin* (1999), a comedy-drama about air traffic controllers. Jolie plays an air traffic controller named Mary Bell. Mike Newell, the movie's director, called Jolie "an extraordinary-looking creature," and likened her to "some weird, undiscovered orchid. She had that little lost bad girl thing which, really, she brought to the part." Newell was impressed that Jolie created much of her character, which was left largely unscripted. "She's a brave, bold girl. I kept checking her age thinking, is she really this young to be this good?"[43]

Actor Billy Bob Thornton plays Mary Bell's husband. Before filming for the movie started, Thornton and Jolie got into the same elevator at the same time one day and were immediately attracted to one another. They seemed to be kindred spirits: Both engaged in many eccentric behaviors. While Jolie was interested in blood and knives, Thornton admitted to many strange phobias, such as a fear of Komodo dragons and antique furniture. At the time, Thornton was engaged to actress Laura Dern, so Jolie and Thornton were initially just friends. The two started having phone conversations several months after finishing *Pushing Tin*.

Jolie, devastated that she could not be with Thornton because of his engagement to Dern, had a nervous breakdown and entered a psychiatric hospital for a few days. Her mother, knowing that Jolie's emotional state had something to do with Thornton, summoned Thornton. Jolie and Thornton became romantically involved shortly thereafter. They married in April 2000; it was her second marriage, his fifth. The two had a low-key (and low-budget) wedding at a chapel in Las Vegas, Nevada. Both dressed casually, wearing jeans, while Thornton wore his trademark ball cap. Much of

Jolie and Billy Bob Thornton met on the movie set of 1999's Pushing Tin. They married in April 2000.

the couple's life played out in public, and the two had many frank conversations with the media about the intimate aspects of their lives, including their sex life and the importance of sharing their blood. Each wore a small vial around their neck that contained the blood of the other. In an interview Thornton explained, "People say they're soul mates, but when you really mean it, you have to prove it, and we give each other our blood."[44]

Doing Life Her Own Way

Jolie considered her relationship with Thornton to be the first one in which she felt normal. As she put it, "if you're at all wild or at all provocative or bold with certain things or not stable in other ways or you have tattoos or knives or whatever it is, [people think] that you can't also be a really caring friend or a really good wife. . . . The great thing I've discovered is that you don't suddenly stabilize and settle down. You do it your own way."[45] Although newly wed, Jolie kept working at her usual, nonstop pace. Unlike many actresses, however, Jolie dismissed the idea that winning an Academy Award meant that she should now accept more serious roles. In fact, she wanted to work on a fun movie next. "I just came out of a mental institution with a bunch of women," she said, talking about her role in *Girl, Interrupted*. "[Now] I want to play with cars; if that means I don't have an image as a 'serious actress' then fine."[46]

Jolie was referring to her next movie choice, *Gone in Sixty Seconds* (2000), an action drama about a car theft ring. Jolie thoroughly enjoyed making the movie. It was fun, and she got to learn how to steal cars. Audiences liked the movie, but critics gave it terrible reviews.

Lara Croft

When the producers of *Lara Croft: Tomb Raider* (2001), a movie about the extremely popular comic strip heroine and fictional video game star Lara Croft, approached Jolie about taking the lead role, she was not interested. She had vivid memories of competing with

In order to embody the iconic Lara Croft character, Jolie had to both mentally and physically prepare for the demanding role.

Croft for her first husband's time. He was addicted to *Tomb Raider*, the video game that features Croft. Jolie also did not like the character because she could not play the game very well. Once she read more about Croft, however, Jolie decided the character was a lot like her: sexy, tough, and adventurous, and she accepted the role.

Playing Lara Croft was tough. She is British, high-class, and has an amazing figure. Indeed, Croft is a female icon to many male gamers—the sexy, buxom, and ready-for-anything Croft is their fantasy woman. Jolie had to play a character that was already well-known and loved, speak with a British accent, and gain 20 pounds (9kg) of muscle. Movie director Simon West recalls preparing Jolie for the role, which required her to learn how to kickbox, use weapons, race with sled dogs, and race on a motorbike. "I knew I was going to have to put Angie through some pretty rigorous training," he said. "I brought her to London and basically put her into boot camp because there were so many different disciplines that she was going to have to learn."[47] Jolie worked out six days a week in a regimen that included yoga, weight training, diving, and cardio workouts. She also ate a special diet and gave up smoking and drinking.

For Jolie, playing Croft became an obsession. She wanted to perform all of her own stunts, which often left the actress bruised, cut, and bleeding. "Jolie ... handles the role's considerable physical demands with aplomb," writes film critic Jack Garner. "Whether she's bouncing from the ceiling on bungee cords or diving off a dam, she makes you believe she does it every day. She's so absolutely right for the role—it's impossible to conceive anyone else doing it."[48]

Although critics thought Jolie nailed the role of Croft, they disliked the fact that the movie capitalized on the popularity of a video game, which they saw as commercial rather than high art. The public, including gamers, however, loved it, and the movie made over $48 million during its debut. Jolie was now a star.

Working on the movie also had another, unexpected impact on Jolie. The movie was filmed in several locations, including England, Cambodia, and Iceland, and when she was in England, Jolie watched the news broadcast by the BBC (British Broadcasting Corporation) and become more familiar with world events. Watching the news as reported by the British also gave her an entirely different perspective on the United States and how it affects the rest of the world. When she was in Cambodia, Jolie became familiar with that poor, underdeveloped country, particularly the plight of its children. Many were malnourished, and some were permanently maimed from land mines that were still in ground from when the country fought its civil war. She vowed to come back and try to help these children.

Finding Maddox

Jolie went on to make two more films, *Original Sin* (2001) and *Life or Something Like It* (2002). Neither was as memorable as *Lara Croft*. But something else was brewing for Jolie. She wanted to take time off from making movies to either have or adopt a baby.

Becoming a mother to baby Maddox, seen here in 2003, in 2001 was a major milestone in Jolie's life.

Thornton had brought two sons from a previous marriage into their marriage, and Jolie and Thornton had always discussed adopting a child or having a child of their own. Jolie was still moved by the children she saw in Cambodia, so the couple decided to adopt. In 2001 they traveled to Cambodia to visit orphanages and found an infant who would eventually become their son, Maddox. Jolie said, "He was asleep. . . . He didn't wake up but they put him in my arms anyway. He opened his eyes and smiled at me. The connection was made that instant."[49]

While Jolie felt a tremendous outpouring of love for the infant, Thornton seemed less enamoured. Right after adopting Maddox, Thornton left on a tour with his rock band. The fact that he would leave the two of them so soon upset Jolie.

Committed to Motherhood

Jolie resumed working, taking the baby with her to movie sets. She was deeply committed to motherhood and grew increasingly disappointed in Thornton's continued lack of interest in the child. Jolie said, "I lost all respect for him and saw that he just wasn't the kind of man I needed or wanted to be with."[50] In 2003 the couple divorced. Thornton took responsibility for the failed marriage. He said, "Nothing was her fault, absolutely nothing. It was all down to me."[51]

Single again and with sole custody of Maddox, Jolie completed filming of a Lara Croft sequel titled *Lara Croft Tomb Raider: The Cradle of Life* and a romantic adventure called *Beyond Borders*. Both movies were released in 2003. In the next phase of her life, however, she focused more on her personal goals.

Chapter 4

Brangelina

Throughout her career, Angelina Jolie has relied on her personal experiences to help her identify with the roles she plays. Known as method acting, this approach has sometimes caused her to blur the lines between her professional and personal lives. She often identifies so much with the characters she plays that she becomes obsessed with them. This seems to also apply to the men that she chooses: All of her relationships, except for her first, have been with her costars. Many of these relationships were over almost as soon as the filming was over, with the exception of one. In *Mr. and Mrs. Smith* (2005) Jolie again mixed her professional and personal lives, this time with costar Brad Pitt. Unlike the others, however, this costar was married, and his wife was Jennifer Aniston, a very popular television star.

Onscreen Chemistry

Despite being a single mom, Jolie remained busy with her career. She had roles in four movies that were all released in 2004: *Taking Lives*, *Sky Captain and the World of Tomorrow*, *Alexander*, and the animated film *Shark Tale*. The most memorable of these roles is "the bad fish" in *Shark Tale*. Jolie remembers when she met her fishy character:

> [The producers] brought me into this room and there were all these different pictures of fish. They were going to explain to me what they wanted me to do and I kind

Working together on the 2005 film **Mr. and Mrs. Smith** *marked the beginning of the Brad Pitt—Angelina Jolie era, later dubbed "Brangelina."*

of looked around . . . and saw this fish with this big red mouth and pointy eyebrows. I thought, 'They can talk as long as they want. I know that I'm THAT fish.' I saw her immediately, I knew it and I liked her. It was me just kind of filling those shoes because they made her very sparkly and sexy.[52]

Also in 2004 Jolie began filming the action-drama *Mr. and Mrs. Smith*, in which she plays Jane Smith, who is married to John Smith, played by Brad Pitt. Jane and John Smith appear to be an average, suburban couple, yet unknown to each other, both work as professional killers. One day each is hired to assassinate the other. The film was a blockbuster hit with moviegoers, and many reviewers noted the chemistry between the two stars. Constance Gorfinkle suggests that their chemistry was as great as that of two other famous actors from the 1930s and 1940s. She writes, "Brad Pitt as John Smith and Angelina Jolie as Jane Smith are absolutely perfect. In fact, they may be the new Cary Grant and Katharine

Hepburn, so wonderfully do they mesh, so ironic and confident are their attitudes. Just looking at them is a treat."[53]

After Jolie and Pitt met on the set of *Mr. and Mrs. Smith*, reporters suggested that the two were spending a lot of time together, even when they were not filming. Rumors circulated that they were romantically involved, even though Jolie stated publicly they were just friends. Pitt, however, soon made some statements in public that hinted at problems in his marriage. Pitt was married at the time to actress Jennifer Aniston, best known for playing Rachel on the hit TV series *Friends*. "Nothing is ever as is seems, is it? I hate the notion of fairy tales anyway," he said. "No one can live up to such a thing. Marriage is tough, it's not easy. There is so much pressure to be with someone forever and I'm not really sure if it's in our nature to be with someone for the rest of our lives."[54] He also told a journalist in April 2004 that "neither of us [he or Aniston] wants to be the spokesman for happy marriage, for coupledom. I despise this two-becomes-one thing, where you lose your individuality."[55]

Yet despite Jolie and Pitt's denials of romance, gossip magazines continued to print stories about them. The alleged Jolie-Pitt union was scandalous, especially because Aniston was a well-loved actress. Her television show, *Friends*, and the character she played, were favorites with the public, which helped her achieve a girl-next-door reputation. Jolie, however, still had a bad-girl reputation. With these public perceptions of the actresses, many people saw Aniston as the victim of the seductive and powerful husband-stealing Jolie. Images of Jolie as a femme fatale and home wrecker dominated the tabloids. Pitt was rather shocked by the vilification of Jolie and defended her against the onslaught. "I've never seen someone so misperceived as Angelina Jolie," he said. "Really, she's surprisingly level-headed and bright, and incredibly decent."[56]

For her part, Jolie continued to adamantly state that her relationship with Pitt was only platonic. She said, "To be intimate with a married man, when my own father cheated on my mother, is not something I could forgive. I could not look at myself in the morning, if I did that."[57]

Brad Pitt

Brad Pitt was born in Shawnee, Oklahoma, on December 18, 1963. He was raised in Springfield, Missouri. He is often described as one of the world's most attractive men. In 1995 *Empire* magazine named him one of the twenty-five sexiest stars in the history of film.

Pitt first gained media attention as the cowboy drifter in the 1991 hit movie *Thelma and Louise*. As his roles got bigger, Pitt quickly gained leading-man status. His many movies include *Legends of the Fall* (1994), *Seven* (1995), *Fight Club* (1999), *Ocean's Eleven* (2001), *Ocean's Twelve* (2004), *Ocean's Thirteen* (2007), *The Curious Case of Benjamin Button* (2008), *Inglourious Basterds* (2009), *Moneyball* (2011), and *World War Z* (2013).

Pitt is also involved in the production side of movie making, and since having children with Jolie, he has become more selective in choosing acting roles. He wants his children to respect and admire his work.

No Longer Just Friends

For a year Jolie and Pitt continued to vow that their relationship was platonic. Meanwhile, the tabloids went wild with the story, reporting that Pitt and Aniston were breaking up, primarily because of Jolie. Pitt and Aniston did break up, and they divorced in 2005. Photos then surfaced showing Pitt playing with Maddox during a vacation with Jolie in Kenya. The two could no longer deny that they were a couple. The tabloids dubbed them "Brangelina" (Brad + Angelina).

By July 2005 Jolie and Pitt were clearly committed to each other. They traveled to Ethiopia, where Jolie adopted an infant girl, naming her Zahara Marley Jolie. The baby's mother died of AIDS, and her father was unknown. In 2006, shortly after the adoption, Pitt and Jolie publicly announced that they were a couple. Even though they did not marry, Pitt adopted Maddox

Pitt and Jolie are pictured with their children Maddox and Zahara in 2006. Though the couple was not married, the children's last names became Jolie-Pitt to demonstrate that they were all a family.

and Zahara, and the couple changed the children's last names to Jolie-Pitt to reflect their new union. Jolie later described how she and Pitt became a couple:

> We were both living, I suppose, very full lives. . . . I think we were the last people who were looking for a relationship.

I certainly wasn't. I was quite content to be a single mom. . . . Because of the film [*Mr. and Mrs. Smith*], we ended up being brought together to do all these crazy things, and I think we found this strange friendship and partnership that kind of just suddenly happened. I think a few months in I realized, "God, I can't wait to get to work." . . . Anything we had to do with each other, we just found a lot of joy in it together and a lot of real teamwork. We just became kind of a pair.[58]

Jolie's description of her relationship with Pitt seems typical of her past relationships. Her costar became her love interest based on the intensity of their roles in their movie. What seemed different in this case, however, was that the relationship seemed more real than imagined, at least in the way Jolie describes the pair's commitment to each other. Jolie says that she and Pitt "spent a lot of time contemplating and thinking and talking about what we both wanted in life and realized that we wanted very similar things."[59]

A New Maturity

In speaking about her new relationship, Jolie seemed to have adopted a new maturity. She was now a mother of two, and this affected her choice of a partner. "Before, I was looking for a friend I could have fun with, be wild with, get lost with," she said. "Now, I'm looking for a man with the same morals as me, the same destiny as me, who can see raising children and approaching the world in the same way. I could never be with a man who was a bad father."[60]

As for Pitt, he seemed to not only fall for Jolie's beauty and charm but also for her dedication to the world's refugees and her commitment to her children. In fact, both Jolie and Pitt think that Maddox played a big role in their fate. Jolie remembers that Maddox "just out of the blue called [Pitt] Dad. It was amazing. We were playing with cars on the floor of a hotel room. . . . That was probably the most defining moment, when [Maddox] decided that we would all be a family."[61]

Jolie's Tattoos

Angelina Jolie has had over a dozen tattoos at one time or another. They include the Tennessee Williams quote, "A prayer for the wild at heart, kept in cages"; the Latin proverb, "Quod me nutrit me destruit," which means "What nourishes me destroys me"; and a large Bengal tiger. To indicate the birthplaces of her children, she has geographical coordinates on her upper left arm (see photo).

Jolie's tattoos, moreover, are ever changing. Several have been changed or removed completely when they were no longer important to her. For example, a blue-tongued dragon that she got on a whim was transformed into a black Latin cross, and a window that was inked on her lower back has since been covered by the tail of the Bengal tiger. Likewise, an Arabic phrase that means "strength of will" was inscribed to cover up an abstract tattoo she got with her ex-husband, Billy Bob Thornton.

Jolie's tattoos have great personal meaning to her.

Pitt also fell for Jolie's sense of adventure and fun. The couple seems to have the kind of relationship that inspires each of them to become better people. Jolie is open about the fact that they compete with one another and in that way make each other better. "He is a great challenge to me," she says. "We push each other to be better. Even if it's just a better bike rider or a better pilot. We're constantly in competition with each other. He's somebody I admire based on the way he lives his life. And that's why I'm with him."[62]

The Good Shepherd

After adopting Zahara, Jolie continued her movie career, but she did not keep as rigorous a filming schedule as she used to. Her next movie was *The Good Shepherd*, released in 2006. The director, Robert De Niro (who is also an Academy Award–winning actor), handpicked the actress for the role of Clover after seeing her in another movie, saying, "She was very good, and kind of tough, but when I watched the scene it made me laugh. I felt that one side of Clover needed that kind of toughness."[63]

The Good Shepherd is about the early years of the Central Intelligence Agency (CIA), a U.S. government agency that collects and evaluates foreign intelligence. Jolie plays the wife of CIA agent Edward Wilson (played by Matt Damon). The character ages several years as the story progresses, and De Niro was worried Jolie could not play the later stage of Clover's life well, because she would need to become aged and frumpy. Yet, in the end, De Niro was pleased with Jolie's performance. "Her instincts are terrific,"[64] he announced.

The Good Shepherd *is a period drama in which Jolie, seen here with fellow actor Matt Damon, had to play a range of ages.*

After *The Good Shepherd*, Jolie worked on two more movies that came out in 2007. First was *Beowulf*, a high-tech animated film based on the medieval epic poem of the same name. Jolie plays the seductive mother of the monster, Grendel. One of the best scenes of the movie is her first appearance, in which she emerges slowly from an underground lake covered in gold body paint. The second movie, *A Mighty Heart*, is based on the book of the same name written by Mariane Pearl. It is about the life and death of Pearl's husband, journalist Daniel Pearl, who was kidnapped and ultimately beheaded by Islamic terrorists in Pakistan in 2002. Jolie plays Mariane Pearl, and she received rave reviews for her performance.

Jolie and Pearl met during the filming of the movie and became good friends. Since Jolie and the other actors were all playing real people, instead of just characters, the scene depicting Pearl's murder was particularly intense. "Maybe it was just the reality that that had happened to a decent man," said Jolie, "but I looked around, and all of them had tears in their eyes. You know, genuinely. It wasn't like a movie set. It felt like we were all remembering a part of something that happened in our lives that we would all be sick about forever."[65]

Bringing this harrowing story to life impacted Jolie's personal outlook, too, helping her to keep her own problems in perspective. "Focusing on that story on a daily basis, you certainly don't worry about your life," she said. "I mean, there isn't a better film to make you hyperaware that you should complain about nothing."[66]

An Upward Career

Jolie then made three movies that were released in 2008. One is the animated movie *Kung Fu Panda*, in which she is the voice of Tigress. In *Wanted* she has a physically demanding role as a seductress who is also capable of performing incredible feats of daring, including racing recklessly around in a red sports car.

In *Changeling* she plays another real-life person, Christine Collins, a single mother whose young son disappears. The police then bring a young boy to Collins and say that he is her missing

*Showing her versatility as an actress, Jolie voices the part of Tigress in the animated **Kung Fu Panda** movies.*

son. Collins knows the child is not her son, even though everyone claims she is just being willful by not recognizing her own child. Collins is torn between taking care of the boy and trying to keep the police on the case of her missing son. They refuse to help her, because they claim the case is solved. Jolie received nominations for a Golden Globe Award and an Academy Award for her performance.

Jolie then moved on to the thriller, *Salt* (2010), in which she has another physically demanding role as a CIA agent. Jolie received good reviews for her performance, but critics did not like the movie. In *The Tourist* (2010) Jolie plays a mysterious woman who meets an American tourist in Italy. The movie was a flop. In *Kung Fu Panda 2* (2011), a sequel to *Kung Fu Panda*, she reprises her role as Tigress.

Jolie had become a successful actress, taking on many demanding roles. She had also become a mother and found a satisfying romantic relationship. In the midst of all this she also found a worthy cause that she could support, and she became known just as much for her humanitarian work as she did for her acting.

Chapter 5

A Humanitarian

Once Jolie's movies brought her wealth and international fame, she began using her celebrity to raise awareness about the plight of the world's refugees. She travels throughout the world and donates millions of dollars to help refugees and displaced persons.

Refugees are people who were forced to leave their homes because of war, violence, natural disaster, or other calamity. They are homeless and in need of all of life's basic necessities. For World Refugee Day (June 20) in 2009, Jolie produced and appeared in a thirty-second, public-service announcement in which she implores viewers not to turn away. She goes on to say, "Refugees are the most vulnerable people on earth. Every day they are fighting to survive. They deserve our respect."[67]

Willing to Learn

While filming *Lara Croft: Tomb Raider* in Angkor, Cambodia, Jolie was shocked by the harsh living conditions of the refugees there. They were victims of a civil war fought throughout the 1970s. She also learned that land mines placed during the war were still in the ground all around the countryside and had maimed and killed unsuspecting children and adults and continued to do so. Jolie recalls, "Cambodia was really eye opening for me."[68]

Interested in learning more about the refugee situation, Jolie contacted the United Nations High Commissioner for Refugees (UNHCR), an agency of the United Nations that helps war refugees with basic needs, such as food and medicine. It also helps them to return to their homes or find new ones in safe

As goodwill ambassador for the United Nations High Commissioner for Refugees Jolie visits with children in a refugee camp in Thailand in 2002.

regions. The organization welcomed Jolie's interest. It knew her fame could attract a lot of attention to refugees. Many other stars, such as former talk-show host Oprah Winfrey and actor Sean Penn, have assisted other causes and charities, and when they did, it helped generate millions of dollars in donations and valuable increased awareness.

In early 2001 Jolie visited UNHCR refugee camps in Sierra Leone, Tanzania, Cambodia, and Pakistan. She was deeply moved by what she saw. In Sierra Leone Jolie was amazed by the resilience of the children in the camps. "The children here grab your hands and walk with you, smiling and singing," she wrote of the experience. "They have nothing. They are wearing ripped dusty clothes and they are smiling. . . . They are so happy to have what little they have now. They are no longer alone or in fear for their safety. Most of them had to walk many, many miles for days with no food or water [to get here]."[69]

During Jolie's goodwill visits to refugee camps, such as this one in Tanzania in 2003, the resilience of the children always amazed her.

In Cambodia she connected with Hazardous Areas Life-Support Organization (HALO), a privately funded, nonprofit organization that removes land mines and other explosives left behind after a war. She also met many people injured by land mines and witnessed for herself the poor conditions in which they lived. Despite what she saw, she cherished the experience. "I have never felt so good in my life," she wrote in her journal at the time. "I am tremendously honored to be with these people. I realize more every day how fortunate I have been in my life. I hope I never forget and never complain again about anything."[70]

In August 2001 the UNHCR named Jolie a goodwill ambassador, and in the following years she continued to visit refugee camps in places such as Namibia, Kenya, Thailand, Ecuador, Darfur, Pakistan, and Iraq as an official representative of the organization. Her fame garnered great attention for the plight

Notes from My Travels

During her first trip to refugee camps in early 2001, Angelina Jolie kept a journal. Later, in 2003, her journal was published as the book, *Notes from My Travels*. In the following excerpt from the introduction to her book, Jolie describes her reaction to visiting the camps and her thoughts about publishing her journal:

I am sure of one thing: I am forever changed. I am so grateful I took this path in my life, thankful that I met these amazing people and had this incredible experience.

I honestly believe that if we were all aware, we would all be compelled to act.

So the question is not how or why I would do this with my life. The question is, how could I not?

. . . I don't know how this [Jolie's journal] will be as a book, how readers will find it. I am not a writer. These are just my journals. They are just a glimpse into a world that I am just beginning to understand, a world I could never really explain in words.

Angelina Jolie. *Notes from My Travels: Visits with Refugees in Africa, Cambodia, Pakistan, and Ecuador.* New York: Pocket Books, 2003, pp. xi–xii.

of refugees. UNHCR spokeswoman Tina Ghelli said, "Thanks to Angelina's involvement, UNHCR is now getting tons of inquiries from young people wanting to help the cause. She has also donated more than a million dollars, and she insists on paying for all of her own expenses on all of her trips."[71] Jolie partly credits her parents for her involvement with the UNHCR. She said, "Both my parents were very focused on charity and I was always raised by my mom to see the joy she had in doing things for others."[72]

Supports Afghan Civilians

On Jolie's visit to Pakistan in early 2001, she viewed the extreme poverty of the area and the plight of Afghan refugees, people from neighboring Afghanistan who had fled to Pakistan to escape the harsh rule of the Taliban in their homeland. The Taliban is an extremist religious group that gave shelter to al Qaeda terrorist Osama bin Laden, the mastermind of the September 11, 2001, terrorist attacks on the United States that killed nearly three thousand people. When the Taliban refused to hand over bin Laden after the attacks, the United States invaded Afghanistan and drove the group from power.

The invasion of Afghanistan was viewed as just retaliation for the September 11 attacks, but Jolie was concerned that Americans would overlook the many Afghans who also hated the Taliban. Indeed, the Afghan people had endured torture and persecution at the hands of the Taliban. She decided to speak out on behalf of Afghan refugees in Pakistan, and she was deeply criticized for her efforts. She even received death threats because of her support of the people in the area. "I went on a [television] show a few days after 9/11 . . . to say that we needed to be focused on the Afghan people, the refugee families," she remembers. "We were focused on the Taliban as an enemy, and these people were their victims too. I got a phone call and two letters that said, very aggressively, how dare I say that we should help anyone else after September 11: 'We should be helping everybody in New York and that's it. . . . I hope your family dies, you're anti-American.'"[73] Jolie was shocked that her concern for Afghan civilians generated such anger in others.

Talking to Victims

One of the places that Jolie has returned to several times is Iraq, where she meets face to face with the displaced people she seeks to help. On one 2007 trip to Iraq, for example, Jolie talked to approximately twelve hundred refugees. She wanted to learn details about their lives so she could share their stories with others.

In 2009 she returned to the region to spend time with families living in makeshift camps northwest of Baghdad. After hearing about their many hardships, including not being able to afford medical treatment, she told one Iraqi, "It takes a lot of strength for you to survive this life. I don't know if I would be strong enough to survive this."[74]

Jolie and Pitt have also traveled to many disaster areas around the world. In 2005 they went to Louisiana after Hurricane Katrina devastated the state, and later that same year they traveled to Pakistan to support the victims of a massive earthquake there.

Jolie visits with displaced families in camps just outside of Baghdad, Iraq, in 2009.

Beyond Goodwill Trips

Jolie's humanitarian work has broadened beyond goodwill trips as she continues to seek out publicity for her causes on a political level. One such effort involves meeting with government officials to advocate for international aid. Since 2003, the actress has met with members of Congress more than twenty times to lobby for her initiatives to help refugees and children.

Meetings with official agencies and organizations followed. In 2005 and 2006 Jolie was invited to speak at the World Economic Forum, a yearly meeting in Switzerland, where political leaders, scholars, and businesspeople come together to discuss issues that affect human health and the environment. In 2007 Jolie became a member of the Council on Foreign Relations, a nonpartisan organization founded in 1921 to promote understanding of foreign policy and America's role in global affairs.

Addressing the G8 Foreign Ministers in 2013 Jolie, in her role as a United Nations humanitarian, speaks out against sexual violence against women during conflict.

Helping in Iraq

In a February 2008 article that she wrote for the *Washington Post* newspaper, Jolie describes the scope of the Iraqi refugee problem and makes an appeal to end the crisis:

We still don't know exactly how many Iraqis have fled their homes, where they've all gone, or how they're managing to survive. Here is what we do know: More than 2 million people are refugees inside their own country—without homes, jobs and, to a terrible degree, without medicine, food or clean water. Ethnic cleansing [the forced relocation or killing of people belonging to a particular ethnic group] and other acts of unspeakable violence have driven them into a vast and very dangerous no-man's land. Many of the survivors huddle in mosques, in abandoned buildings with no electricity, in tents or in one-room huts made of straw and mud. Fifty-eight percent of these internally displaced people are younger than 12 years old. . . .

My visit left me even more deeply convinced that we not only have a moral obligation to help displaced Iraqi families, but also a serious, long-term, national security interest in ending this crisis.

Angelina Jolie. "Staying to Help in Iraq." *Washington Post*, February 28, 2008. www.washingtonpost.com/wp-dyn/content/article/2008/02/27/AR2008022702217.html.

Raising Money

Like many of Hollywood's top actresses, Jolie commands a large salary for her movie roles. Jolie feels good when she uses the millions she earns to fund the causes closest to her heart. In fact, her humanitarian work is a main reason that she continues to act. "I'm able to take the money and see a hospital built or build a well somewhere," she said. "It makes me all that more eager to go to work and be successful because I know I can do good things."[75]

One way Jolie uses her fame to raise money is by requiring that she be paid for interviews and for photo shoots with her or her children; she then donates that money to charity. Another way was to write a book. *Notes from My Travels*, a collection of entries from the journal that she kept during her first trip to refugee camps, was published in 2003. Jolie donates all the profits from her book to the UNHCR.

In the book's foreword, Ruud Lubbers, the United Nations High Commissioner for Refugees, writes, "[Jolie] has proven to be a close partner and a genuine colleague in our efforts to find solutions for the world's refugees. Above all, she has helped to make the tragedy of refugees real to everyone who will listen. Angelina's interest in helping refugees, her personal generosity, and her truly compassionate spirit are an inspiration to us all."[76]

Her Own Charitable Foundations

Jolie believes that adopting a child from another country establishes not just a commitment to the child but also to the child's country of origin. For that reason, after Jolie adopted Maddox in Cambodia in 2002, she built a primitive home in northern Cambodia. It is in a remote location and requires travel by air, sea, and car to reach it. Then in 2003 Jolie created the Maddox Jolie Project (MJP), a conservation and community development program in Cambodia. After Jolie and Pitt changed Maddox's last name from Jolie to Jolie-Pitt in 2006, Jolie renamed the program the Maddox Jolie-Pitt Foundation. According to the foundation's website, the MJP

> is committed to environmental security, creating peace and stability in all communities by planning and implementing interventions that prevent negative environmental changes. Working with impoverished rural villagers and local governments to alleviate food insecurities and increase access to basic primary healthcare and education, we're implementing projects that build healthy and vibrant communities.[77]

Among its many projects, the MJP opened a health-care center to provide services to more than five thousand villagers in rural

Cambodia. Since it opened its doors in October 2009, the center has served over nine thousand villagers and is the most-visited clinic in the region.

Jolie works through the MJP to provide aid and fund programs far beyond Cambodia. For example, the MJP funded a wildlife sanctuary in Namibia for the care of injured wildlife. Jolie also funded children's health centers in Cambodia and Ethiopia so that they can provide innovative treatment to children infected with HIV/AIDS and tuberculosis. The organization also donated $1 million to Doctors Without Borders, an international medical humanitarian organization founded in 1971.

In 2008 Jolie partnered with Microsoft, a software company, to create Kids in Need of Defense (KIND), which provides legal help for refugee or immigrant children who come to the United States from other countries alone, without a parent or guardian. More than eight thousand unaccompanied children come to the United States every year to escape abuse, persecution, war, and other dangers. KIND finds lawyers to represent these children for free and to help prevent them from being sent back to countries where they will be in danger. KIND also works to change U.S. laws and policies to better protect these children.

"The Greatest Privilege"

Jolie's humanitarian efforts have garnered lots of attention, and she has been honored with many awards for her work. In 2003 Jolie was the first recipient of the Citizen of the World Award given by the United Nations Correspondents' Association. The award honors people who have made a significant contribution to humanitarian causes. Jolie was honored again in 2005 when she received the United Nations Global Humanitarian Action Award for her work on behalf of the United Nations. As she received the award, she noted, "Second to my children, spending time with refugees has been the greatest privilege."[78]

Also in 2005, Jolie was awarded Cambodian citizenship by Cambodia's king Norodom Sihamoni for her many contributions there. Two years later, Jolie, along with United Nations

Jolie is presented with the Citizen of the World Award, given by the United Nations Correspondents' Association, in 2003.

High Commissioner for Refugees, António Guterres, received the Freedom Award from the International Rescue Committee in honor of their humanitarian contributions.

In October 2011 the UNHCR paid a special tribute to Jolie in honor of her ten years of service as a UNHCR goodwill ambassador. Guterres also asked her to take on an expanded role of a special envoy to very intense, dramatic refugee situations. Guterres hoped Jolie's high-profile status could raise awareness about the refugees' plight. "We will all be counting not only [on] your commitment but also your diplomatic [skills] and your vision and insights on how to help solve some of the most complex problems that we face together with the international community,"[79] he said.

Jolie believes that her humanitarian efforts and her role as a mother will be her most long-lived accomplishments. Although she continues to receive accolades for her acting, Jolie would most like to be remembered for her work as a goodwill ambassador and her efforts to aid people worldwide.

Chapter 6

A Power Mom

While her career and her humanitarian work was immensely important to her, Angelina Jolie found that it was her own children who made the biggest difference in her life. In 2007 she said,

> I'm committed to the future now. I'm committed to life. I think definitely before my son [Maddox], I was a little nihilistic [believed that life is meaningless]. But once I adopted [Maddox] I knew I was never going to be intentionally self-destructive again. I'm starting to be able to see being 50 years old with the kids graduating from high school—though in my mind we're in the middle of a desert or a jungle with tutors and some local friends."[80]

Biological Children

In January 2006 Jolie and Pitt stunned the media when they announced that Jolie was pregnant. She had previously said that with so many children around the world in need of a family, she was not sure if she ever wanted to have her own children. She explained her change of mind this way: "Before I met Brad, I always said I was happy never to have a child biologically. He told me he hadn't given up that thought. Then, a few months after [Zahara] came home, I saw Brad with her and [Maddox], and I realised how much he loved them, that a biological child would not in any way be a threat. So I said, I want to try."[81]

Jolie arriving at the London Aquarium with four of her six children, Shiloh, Knox, Vivienne and Zahara, in 2011 in London, England.

The couple decided to have their baby in the African nation of Namibia. Jolie and Pitt both felt that the country's remoteness would offer them privacy during the pregnancy and birth. On May 27, 2006, Jolie gave birth to a girl, Shiloh Nouvel Jolie-Pitt, in a tiny Namibian hospital. "We aren't completely insane," said Jolie about her willingness to entrust her care to a hospital in a small, third-world country. "We looked for places that were not rife with malaria and dengue fever, and Namibia is good for that because it's so dry."[82] Days after Shiloh's birth, Jolie and Pitt donated three hundred thousand dollars to two hospitals in Namibia so they could improve their maternity wards. Two months later, the couple returned to the United States, where they were greeted by a frenzy of reporters and photographers.

Many people were curious about how Jolie now felt about having a biological child, assuming that she would feel more deeply toward her biological child than her adopted children. But Jolie surprised many people by stating, "I found the opposite. I feel so much more for [Maddox] and [Zahara] because they are survivors, they came through so much. Shiloh seemed so privileged from the moment she was born, I have less inclination to feel for her."[83]

The very next year, in 2007, Jolie and Pitt adopted Pax, a three-and-a-half-year-old Vietnamese orphan. Jolie said that he cried at first, but she held him and talked to him. "By day three, he didn't want me to put him down. I think he got used to the reality that somebody loves you and that's what a mother is."[84]

Jolie was soon pregnant again. In 2008 she gave birth to twins, Knox Leon and Vivienne Marcheline, in France. The twins brought the family's total to eight, and both Jolie and Pitt have stated they may not be done yet. As she told *Marie Claire* magazine in 2011, "nothing [is] planned at the moment, but we just don't know. I could end up pregnant."[85] Pitt's desire to be part of a large family dates back to when he was a child. "I had a friend who had a big family when I was a kid," he said. "I just loved the chaos. . . . I just decided then if I was ever going to do it—this left some indelible mark on me—if I was ever going to do it, that's the way I was going to do it."[86]

The Family Influence

Jolie and Pitt take pride in how they handle their family and their careers, and they have been vocal about the pleasure they derive from family and the ways in which they work together. For example, the couple's golden rule is that one parent will always be

Savvy Businesspeople

While Angelina Jolie and Brad Pitt may be actors and humanitarians, they are also savvy businesspeople. They understand their own popularity, and in 2006 they used their celebrity to negotiate a whopping $4.1 million from *People* magazine for the first photographs of newborn Shiloh. They promptly gave the entire amount to charity. Two years later, the first pictures of infant twins Vivienne and Knox hit the newsstands, again in *People*. The fee for the twins' photos was close to $14 million dollars, and the money also went to charity.

Exclusive photos of twins Knox and Vivienne earned Jolie and Pitt $14 million, all of which went to charity.

In an interview with National Public Radio, Pitt describes why the couple decided to sell photos of their children and how hard it is to avoid the paparazzi (aggressive photographers who chase celebrities to get a photo):

It's a very strange thing to be selling photos of something that's very intimate and personal. And those of which you want to protect. We have to plan an escape every day just to get out of the house—kind of a Mission Impossible with decoys, and that's the life we live in, and that's the one we asked for. But we knew there was a bounty on our head . . . and we know the lengths they (the paparazzi) go to get that shot [photo]. So we figured, 'Let's cut it off in the beginning,' and instead of that money going to people I do not respect, we would make some good out of it.

Quoted in National Public Radio. "Brad Pitt: 'Moneyball,' Life and 'The Stalkerazzi.'" NPR, September 22, 2011. www.npr.org/2011/09/22/140629778/brad-pitt-moneyball-life-and-the-stalkerazzi.

at home with the six children. Joile says, "We take turns working. One of us is always at home with the kids—*always*. Taking them out to things and being there with them and bringing them to school or to the set to visit Mommy or Daddy."[87] The two relish the home role so much, they often compete over it. Jolie says, "We both, like most people, we like being home. Whoever is the one who is home tends to be the happier one because we get to play with the kids and the other one is out earning the money."[88]

The couple defines the word *home* loosely, as they are continuously on the move, wherever their movie roles take them. Jolie and Pitt pride themselves on their nomadic lifestyle as they settle in and take over a rented house or the floor of a hotel for a few weeks while filming. Jolie claims that the children also like being on the move and will ask where they are going next if the family remains at home for more than a month. Jolie and Pitt also own a home in several places, including France; Cambodia; New Orleans, Louisiana; and Los Angeles, California.

Their commitment to family influences the roles both Jolie and Pitt choose to take. For example, Jolie accepted the role in *The Tourist* (2010) because "I was looking for a very short thing to do before Brad started filming [*Moneyball* (2011)] . . . and I said I needed something that shoots not too long, in a nice location for my family. Somebody said there's a script that's been around, and it shoots in Venice and Paris."[89]

Both Jolie and Pitt want roles that will be inspirational to their children. Pitt expressed this after filming *The Tree of Life* (2011), an intense drama that explores the meaning of life through a Texas man's childhood memories. "If I'm choosing a film now, I want it to be maybe less immature than things I have done in the past," said Pitt. "I'm very conscious, when they're adults I want it to mean something to them. I want them to think, 'Dad's alright.'"[90]

Parenting Style

Jolie and Pitt clearly believe in their family and in making it a priority. They readily compliment one another on their parenting abilities and claim that working as a team is the key to making it all work. They also believe in allowing their children to express themselves. For example, Shiloh likes to dress as a boy, wear her hair like a boy's, and be called "John." When asked about her daughter's overly tomboyish characteristics, Jolie is unconcerned. She says, "Some kids wear capes and want to be Superman and she wants to be like her brothers. It's who she is."[91] They have also allowed Maddox to have a dagger collection, similar to the one Jolie had when she was a teenager.

Goals that Jolie and Pitt have for their children include ensuring that they learn about the culture of their country of origin and that there are less fortunate people in the world who need help. Teaching the children about their countries of origin and having respect for other cultures extends to their nannies—each child has a nanny with a different cultural background. One nanny speaks Vietnamese to Pax and Cambodian to Maddox. The children have flags over their beds from their countries of origin. "They are all learning about each other's cultures as well as being proud of their own," said Jolie. "So it's not like just the boys get to do the Asian thing. They all have their flags over their beds and their individual pride."[92]

The Jolie-Pitt Homes

Angelina Jolie and Brad Pitt own homes across the globe, including their main home in Los Angeles, California, and a small home in New Orleans, Louisiana, where Pitt helps run a nonprofit project to build homes for the victims of Hurricane Katrina. The family also enjoys their home in Cambodia, in part because they want to give their children a global experience, and also because it is one of the few places where they can enjoy some respite from the ever-present paparazzi.

The couple's largest property is a sprawling chateau in the tiny village of Brignoles in Provence, France. The luxurious property, which is classified as a historic monument, includes a swimming pool, twenty fountains, a lake, and numerous fields surrounded by a huge forest. Pitt, an architecture enthusiast, is overseeing extensive renovations that will add modern comforts to the estate, which was built in the fourteenth century.

Though they are two of the most famous Hollywood stars today, Jolie and Pitt place the highest priority on keeping family first.

Jolie sees travel as a way to reinforce lessons about culture and history. Whenever they travel, Jolie makes sure her children see the important historical sites of each country and that they do typical tourist activities so they can learn about the places they visit. She wants them to learn about history "right." "I don't want

At the December 2011 New York premiere of In the Land of Blood and Honey *Jolie poses with two of its stars, Zana Marjanovic, left, and Goran Kostic, second from left.*

Zahara to learn about being an African woman by learning about slavery first,"[93] she points out.

New Frontiers

Beyond being a devoted mother, Jolie involves herself in new activities that interest her. In 2011 she made her directorial debut with the movie *In the Land of Blood and Honey*, a film depicting a love story set against the background of the Bosnian Civil War of 1992–1995.

Jolie also wrote the script. Writing a movie script was something that she always wanted to do, but she never had the opportunity. Jolie says that writing the script for *In the Land of Blood and Honey* began as "an excuse to get out some of my frustrations [with] the international community and justice issues. I just assumed nobody would ever see or read it."[94] She began reading it to Pitt and then to some of her friends, and their enthusiasm for it encouraged her to finish it. Once she had so much invested, Jolie wanted to direct the movie herself.

She was so concerned about the authenticity of the movie that it was not until after the actors had read the script and filming began that Jolie revealed she was the author. Many of the actors were amazed. "I was really shocked to find out that someone who was not in the war knows so much about it," said Boris Ler, a Sarajevan actor who plays Tarik. "She gets what people were feeling during that time."[95]

The movie is unusual for many reasons. Jolie filmed it in Hungary and Bosnia in just forty-two days. She chose a cast of local Bosnian and Serbian actors and actresses who had personally lived through the war. She filmed the entire movie twice, once in English and once in the languages of the region, Bosnian, Serbian and Croatian. And, in addition to hiring local actors, Jolie also hired locals to help in the production, housing, and feeding of the cast and crew. She says her goal with the movie was not to take a political side but to "open up a discussion and make sure no one forgets."[96]

Critics mostly praised *In the Land of Blood and Honey*, describing it as gripping and moving. Several praised Jolie for taking on such a serious topic as her first directing effort and suggested that

Jolie received the Honorary Award for Opposing War and Genocide for her film In the Land of Blood and Honey *at the Cinema for Peace charity event in 2012.*

A Devastating Loss

In 2007 Angelina Jolie suffered a devastating loss when her mother, Marcheline Bertrand, died after a seven-year battle with ovarian and breast cancer. Jolie was always close to her mother, and her death hit Jolie hard. In a joint statement, she and her brother, James, said, "There are no words to express what an amazing woman and mother she was. She was our best friend."[1]

Jolie immersed herself in her children to cope with her mother's death. Jolie had always drawn inspiration as a mother from her own mother, and after her mother's death, she worried that she was lacking in comparison. "I will never be as good a mother as she was," said Jolie. "She was just grace incarnate. She was the most generous, loving—she's better than me."[2]

1. Quoted in Mike Parker. "Angelina Jolie: I Will Marry Brad Pitt." *Express*, February 4, 2007. www.express.co.uk/posts/view/1884/Angelina-Jolie-I-WILL-marry-Brad-Pitt.
2. Quoted in CBS News. "Angelina Jolie: Behind the Camera." *60 Minutes*, November 27, 2011. www.cbsnews.com/8301-18560_162-57330673/angelina-jolie-behind-the-camera.

she might have a career in directing if she chose. Andrew Pulver of the *Guardian* newspaper writes, "*In the Land of Blood and Honey* is impressive in its lack of directorial flourishes: it feels like a film borne out of scrupulous research and deeply felt conviction."[97] Peter Travers of *Rolling Stone* magazine writes, "It's as a director that Jolie shines. She gets strong, stinging performances from [her actors]. . . . Jolie has a keen eye for the core of a scene and a true director's instinct for the pulse that defines character."[98]

A Life-Changing Decision

In May 2013 Jolie made a stunning announcement that had nothing to do with her acting or directing careers, but rather was very personal. Writing in a *New York Times* article, Jolie divulged that in early 2013 she had chosen to undergo a preventive double mastectomy (the surgical removal of both breasts) in order to significantly reduce her chances of getting breast cancer in the future. Jolie writes, "The truth is I carry a "faulty" gene, BRCA1, which sharply increases my risk of developing breast cancer and ovarian cancer.... Once I knew that this was my reality, I decided to be proactive and to minimize the risk as much I could."[99]

Though Jolie had not been diagnosed with breast cancer at the time of the surgery, she felt the procedure was the right choice for her, especially since her own mother had battled ovarian and breast cancer for years and eventually succumbed to the disease in 2007 at age 56. "I wanted to write this [article] to tell other women that the decision to have a mastectomy was not easy. But it is one I am very happy that I made," Jolie says. "[As a result of the surgery] my chances of developing breast cancer have dropped from 87 percent to under 5 percent." Jolie acknowledges that breast removal is not the only option for women with the BRCA1 gene, and that every woman, along with her doctors, must do what is right for her. "For any woman reading this, I hope it helps you to know you have options. I want to encourage every woman, especially if you have a family history of breast or ovarian cancer, to seek out the information and medical experts who can help you through this aspect of your life, and to make your own informed choices."[100] In the future Jolie may elect to remove her ovaries as a preventive measure against ovarian cancer, which has an elevated risk when the BRCA1 gene is present.

Even after a surgery as serious as a double mastectomy, Jolie continues her demanding roles as an actress and a director. For Jolie, however, her most important jobs are as a mother and as a citizen of the world. In the end, Jolie hopes her legacy will be that she helped to improve the lives of people everywhere. She said, "I love being able to tell a good story or just to entertain, and I don't look down upon it. It's just that at the end of the day, when I die, I feel that the more significant contribution to have made would be to save a life or change a law that's going to affect people and their children and their country and their rights in the future."[101]

Introduction: Committed to Life

1. Quoted in Michael Angeli. "Angelina Jolie: Tres Jolie." *Movieline*, March 1, 1999. www.movieline.com/1999/03/01/ angelina-jolie-tres-jolie/3.
2. Quoted in Ron Redmond. "Angelina Jolie Appeals for More Afghan Returnee Support After Visit." UNHCR: The UN Refugee Agency, October 24, 2008. www.unhcr.org/ 4901b8464.html.
3. Quoted in Mike Goodridge. "Mother Angelina." *Evening Standard* (London), June 15, 2007. www.thisislondon .co.uk/showbiz/article-23400606-mother-angelina.do.
4. Quoted in Dana Kennedy. "Angelina Jolie Happy to Talk About Adoption with Her Kids." *People*, May 14, 2011. www.people.com/people/article/0,,20488864,00.html.

Chapter 1: A Life Apart

5. Quoted in Independent.ie. "Angelina Overdoes the Bad Girl Act." Independent.ie, October 18, 2001. www.independent .ie/lifestyle/independent-woman/celebrity-news-gossip/ angelina-overdoes-the-bad-girl-act-329898.html.
6. Quoted in Independent.ie. "Angelina Overdoes the Bad Girl Act."
7. Quoted in Chris Heath. "Blood, Sugar, Sex, Magic." *Rolling Stone*, July 5, 2001. http://pages.citebite.com/ v1k6y5x9n4fqv.
8. Quoted in Rhona Mercer. *Angelina Jolie: The Biography*. London: John Blake, 2007, p. 3.
9. Quoted in Independent.ie. "Angelina Overdoes the Bad Girl Act."
10. Quoted in "Angelina Jolie Voight," June 13, 2011. http:// lifestylemagazine.biz/angelina-jolie-voight/.

11. Quoted in Todd Gold. "Lip Service." *People*, May 24, 2004. www.people.com/people/archive/article/0,,20150150,00.html.
12. Quoted in Mercer. *Angelina Jolie*, p. 4.
13. Quoted in Mercer. *Angelina Jolie*, p. 8.
14. Quoted in Heath. "Blood, Sugar, Sex, Magic."
15. Quoted in *Cosmopolitan*. "Angelina Jolie: What You Never Knew...Until Now!" *Cosmopolitan*. www.cosmopolitan.com/celebrity/exclusive/angelina-jolie.
16. Quoted in Sharon Feinstein. "Angelina's Secret Sadness—by Her Brother." MailOnline, March 26, 2007. www.dailymail.co.uk/tvshowbiz/article-444390/Angelinas-secret-sadness--brother.html.
17. Quoted in Nancy Jo Sales. "Sex and the Single Mom." *Vanity Fair*, June 2005. www.vanityfair.com/hollywood/features/2005/06/angelina-jolie-200506.
18. Quoted in Heath. "Blood, Sugar, Sex, Magic."
19. Quoted in Mercer. *Angelina Jolie*, p. 18.
20. Quoted in *Paula Zahn Now*. CNN, June 9, 2005. http://transcripts.cnn.com/TRANSCRIPTS/0506/09/pzn.01.html.
21. Quoted in "Jolie: 'Troubled Teens Should Visit Africa.'" Contactmusic.com, June 29, 2005. http://www.contactmusic.com/news-article/jolie-troubled-teens-should-visit-africa.

Chapter 2: A Turbulent Start

22. Quoted in Mercer. *Angelina Jolie*, p. 26.
23. Quoted in Independent.ie. "Angelina Overdoes the Bad Girl Act."
24. Quoted in *Empire*. "Jonny Lee Miller and Angelina Jolie—the Happy Couple." June 1996. http://angelanna3.tripod.com/interviews/id1.html.
25. Quoted in Mercer. *Angelina Jolie*, p. 26.
26. Quoted in Mercer. *Angelina Jolie*, p. 26.
27. Quoted in Gary Dretzka. "Angelina Jolie Warily Regards Rising Fame." *Chicago Tribune*, September 4, 1996. http://articles.chicagotribune.com/1996-09-

04/features/9609040298_1_intimate-film-independent-films-mike-figgis/2.

28. Quoted in Mercer. *Angelina Jolie*, p. 28.

29. Hal Hinson. "Hackers." *Washington Post*, September 15, 1995. http://www.washingtonpost.com/wp-srv/style/longterm/movies/videos/hackersrhinson_c02d40.htm.

30. Roger Ebert. "Hackers." *Chicago Sun-Times*, September 15, 1995. http://rogerebert.suntimes.com/apps/pbcs.dll/article?AID=/19950915/REVIEWS/509150302.

31. Quoted in Dretzka. "Angelina Jolie Warily Regards Rising Fame."

32. Quoted in Heath. "Blood, Sugar, Sex, Magic."

33. Quoted in Angeli. "Angelina Jolie: Tres Jolie."

34. Quoted in *People*. "Celebrity Central: Angelina Jolie." *People*. www.people.com/people/angelina_jolie/biography.

35. Quoted in *Empire*. "Jonny Lee Miller and Angelina Jolie—the Happy Couple."

Chapter 3: A Successful Actress

36. Quoted in Diane Anderson. "Tis the Season to Be Jolie." *Girlfriends*, December 1997. http://angelanna3.tripod.com/interviews/id4.html.

37. Quoted in Kathleen Tracy. *Angelina Jolie: A Biography*. Santa Barbara, CA: Greenwood, 2008, p. 46.

38. Roger Ebert. Review of *Playing by Heart*. *Chicago Sun-Times*, January 22, 1999. http://rogerebert.suntimes.com/apps/pbcs.dll/article?AID=/19990122/REVIEWS/901220304/1023.

39. James Berardinelli. Review of *Playing by Heart*. Reelviews. www.reelviews.net/php_review_template.php?identifier=1839.

40. Quoted in *Girl, Interrupted*. Directed by James Mangold. Culver City, CA: Sony Pictures Home Entertainment, 2000. DVD.

41. James Brundage. Review of *Girl, Interrupted*. Filmcritic.com, January 15, 2000. www.imdb.com/reviews/226/22679.html.

42. Quoted in *Girl, Interrupted*.

43. Quoted in Alison Boleyn. "Celebrity Profile: Angelina Jolie." *Marie Claire*, February 2000. http://ajolie.hollywood.com/int13.html.

44. Quoted in Stephen Schaefer. "Billy Bob Bound to Angelina by Blood." ABC News, May 14, 2001. http://abcnews.go.com/Entertainment/story?id=105269&page=1.

45. Quoted in Heath. "Blood, Sugar, Sex, Magic."

46. Quoted in Mercer. *Angelina Jolie*, p. 110.

47. Quoted in "Crafting Lara Croft." *Lara Croft: Tomb Raider*. Directed by Simon West. Los Angeles: Paramount Pictures, 2001. DVD, Special Collector's Edition.

48. Jack Garner. "'Tomb Raider' Succeeds Where Other Movies Based on Video Games Fail." *Army Times*, June 15, 2001. www.armytimes.com/legacy/rar/1-213098-363665.php.

49. Quoted in Louis B. Hobson. "The Jolly Life of Angelina." *Calgary Sun*, July 20, 2003.

50. Quoted in Mercer. *Angelina Jolie*, p. 152.

51. Quoted in Garth Franklin. "Interview: Angelina Jolie for 'Sky Captain.'" Dark Horizons, September 8, 2004. www.darkhorizons.com/features/1083/angelina-jolie-for-sky-captain.

Chapter 4: Brangelina

52. Quoted in Andrew Buncombe. "Angelina Jolie: The Maneater—or a Victim of Hypocrisy?" *Independent* (London), January 15, 2005. www.independent.co.uk/news/people/profiles/angelina-jolie-the-maneater-or-a-victim-of-hypocrisy-6154838.html.

53. Constance Gorfinkle. "Drop Dead Gorgeous—Brad Pitt, Angelina Jolie Make a Sexy and Secretive Couple in 'Mr. and Mrs. Smith.'" *Quincy (MA) Patriot Ledger*, June 10, 2005.

54. Quoted in Mercer. *Angelina Jolie*, p. 231.

55. Quoted in Mercer. *Angelina Jolie*, p. 231.

56. Quoted in *Chicago Tribune*. "'I've Never Seen Someone So Misperceived as Angelina.'" May 6, 2004. http://articles.chicagotribune.com/2004-05-06/news/0405070049_1_co-star-mrs-smith-redeye.

57. Angelina Jolie. "'Do I Need to Defend That I'm a Decent Woman?'" Interview by Anne Curry. *Today*, June 8, 2005. http://today.msnbc.msn.com/id/8116437/ns/today-entertainment/t/do-i-need-defend-im-decent-woman/#.TxIbtm_pF2A.

58. Quoted in Jonathan Van Meter. "The Bold and the Beautiful." *Vogue*, January 2007. http://www.homunculus.com/articles/jolieangelina/jolie200701vogue.html.

59. Quoted in Van Meter. "The Bold and the Beautiful."

60. Quoted in Michelle Lopez. "I Just Naturally Don't Rely on Men." *Mail on Sunday* (London), January 2, 2005.

61. Quoted in Van Meter. "The Bold and the Beautiful."

62. Quoted in Van Meter. "The Bold and the Beautiful."

63. Quoted in Van Meter. "The Bold and the Beautiful."

64. Quoted in Van Meter. "The Bold and the Beautiful."

65. Quoted in Chris Connelly. "Angelina Unbound." *Marie Claire*, June 8, 2007. www.marieclaire.com/celebrity-lifestyle/celebrities/angelina-jolie-4.

66. Quoted in Connelly. "Angelina Unbound."

Chapter 5: A Humanitarian

67. Quoted in UNHCR: The UN Refugee Agency. "Angelina Jolie Releases New Video to Draw Attention to Plight of Refugees Around the World." Press release. June 16, 2009. www.unhcr.org/4a37a0466.html.

68. Quoted in Laura La Bella. *Angelina Jolie: Goodwill Ambassador for the United Nations*. New York: Rosen, 2009, p. 11.

69. Angelina Jolie. *Notes from My Travels: Visits with Refugees in Africa, Cambodia, Pakistan, and Ecuador*. New York: Pocket Books, 2003, pp. 26–27.

70. Jolie. *Notes from My Travels*, p. 103.

71. Quoted in *Cosmopolitan*. "Angelina Jolie."

72. Quoted in Goodridge. "Mother Angelina."

73. Quoted in WENN.com. "Angelina Jolie Stunned by Post-9/11 Death Threats." Hollywood, May 23, 2007. www.hollywood.com/news/Jolie_Stunned_by_Post_911_Death_Threats/3701301.

74. Quoted in *Us Weekly*. "Angelina Jolie Makes Third Trip to Iraq." *Us Weekly*, July 23, 2009. www.usmagazine.com/celebrity-news/news/angelina-jolie-makes-third-trip-to-iraq-2009237.

75. Quoted in Gavin Esler. "Angelina Jolie—An Actor on a Mission?" BBC News, December 4, 2004. http://news.bbc.co.uk/2/hi/programmes/hardtalk/4098423.stm.

76. Ruud Lubbers. Foreword to *Notes from My Travels*, p. x.

77. Maddox Jolie-Pitt Foundation. "At a Glance." Maddox Jolie-Pitt Foundation. www.mjpasia.org.

78. Quoted in UN News Centre. "UN Refugee Agency Goodwill Ambassador Angelina Jolie Honoured by UNA-USA." UN News Centre, October 12, 2005. www.un.org/apps/news/storyAr.asp?NewsID=16191&Cr=refuge&Cr1=.

79. Quoted in UNHCR: The UN Refugee Agency. "Angelina Jolie Appeals to Governments to Step Up Life-Saving Efforts in the Horn of Africa." UNHCR: The UN Refugee Agency, October 4, 2011. www.unhcr.org/4e8b19c09.html.

Chapter 6: A Power Mom

80. Quoted in Van Meter. "The Bold and the Beautiful."

81. Quoted in Sara Davidson. "Face to Face with Angelina Jolie." *Reader's Digest*, July 2007. www.readersdigest.com.au/rd-face-to-face-angelina-jolie.

82. Quoted in Van Meter. "The Bold and the Beautiful."

83. Quoted in Mercer. *Angelina Jolie*, p. 255.

84. Quoted in Davidson. "Face to Face with Angelina Jolie."

85. Quoted in Chris Connelly. "Unstoppable Angelina." *Marie Claire*, December 13, 2011. www.marieclaire.com/celebrity-lifestyle/celebrities/angelina-jolie-interview.

86. Quoted in Lori Smith. "People: Pitt Says I Know Big Family 'Seems Extreme.'" *Denver Post*, May 19, 2011. www.denverpost.com/lifestyles/ci_18087510.

87. Quoted in Vicki Woods. "The Other Angelina." *Vogue*, November 10, 2010. www.vogue.com/magazine/article/december-cover-angelina-jolie/?mbid=ob_ppc_139#1.

88. Quoted in Woods. "The Other Angelina."
89. Quoted in Woods. "The Other Angelina."
90. Brad Pitt. "Being Brad." Interview by Tara Brown. *60 Minutes*, November 11, 2011. http://sixtyminutes.ninemsn.com.au/article.aspx?id=8372953.
91. Quoted in Martyn Palmer. "'The Skeletons Have Already Been Let Out of My Closet': Angelina Jolie Reveals the Truth About Brad and Her Children." MailOnline, December 6, 2010. www.dailymail.co.uk/home/you/article-1334402/Angelina-Jolie-reveals-truth-Brad-Pitt-children.html.
92. Quoted in Matthew Garrahan. "Lunch with the FT: Angelina Jolie." *Financial Times*, July 29, 2011. www.ft.com/cms/s/2/c7a3b56c-b90e-11e0-bd87-00144feabdc0.html#axzz1l3y5depl.
93. Quoted in Ramin Setoodeh. "Angelina Jolie Discusses New Film and Humanitarian Work with Tina Brown." Daily Beast, December 5, 2011. www.thedailybeast.com/articles/2011/12/05/angelina-jolie-discusses-new-film-and-humanitarian-work-with-tina-brown.html.
94. Quoted in Connelly. "Unstoppable Angelina."
95. Quoted in Steven Zeitchik. "'Blood and Honey' Opens Painful Window to Past for Some in Cast." *Los Angeles Times*, December 24, 2011. http://articles.latimes.com/2011/dec/24/entertainment/la-et-angelina-jolie-20111224.
96. Quoted in Zeitchik. "'Blood and Honey' Opens Painful Window to Past for Some in Cast."
97. Peter Travers. Review of *In the Land of Blood and Honey*. *Rolling Stone*, December 29, 2011. http://www.rollingstone.com/movies/reviews/in-the-land-of-blood-and-honey-20111229.
98. Andrew Pulver. Review of *In the Land of Blood and Honey*. *Guardian*, February 10, 2012. http://www.guardian.co.uk/film/2012/feb/10/in-the-land-blood-honey-review.
99. Angelina Jolie. "My Medical Choice." *The New York Times*, May 14, 2013. http://www.nytimes.com/2013/05/14/opinion/my-medical-choice.html?_r=0
100. Jolie. "My Medical Choice."
101. Quoted in Goodridge. "Mother Angelina."

1975

Angelia Jolie Voight is born on June 4 in Los Angeles, California.

1976

Jolie's parents separate.

1980

Jolie's parents divorce.

1982

Jolie appears in her first movie, *Lookin' to Get Out*.

1986

Jolie enrolls in the Lee Strasberg Theatre and Film Institute.

1991

At the age of 16, Jolie gets a job as a model at Finesse Model Management; she appears in several MTV music videos, including *Rock 'n' Roll Dreams Come Through* and *Anybody Seen My Baby?*

1993

Jolie appears in the movie *Cyborg 2*.

1995

Jolie appears in the movies *Without Evidence* and *Hackers*.

1996

Jolie appears in the movies *Mojave Moon, Love Is All There Is*, and *Foxfire*; she marries actor Jonny Lee Miller.

1997

Jolie appears in the movies *Playing God, True Women*, and *George Wallace*.

1998

Jolie receives a Golden Globe Award for her performance in *George Wallace* (1997); she appears in the movies *Gia*, *Hell's Kitchen*, and *Playing by Heart*.

1999

Jolie and Miller divorce; she receives a Golden Globe Award for her performance in *Gia* (1998); she appears in the movies *Pushing Tin*; *The Bone Collector*; and *Girl, Interrupted*.

2000

Jolie marries actor Billy Bob Thornton; she receives a Golden Globe Award and an Academy Award for her performance in *Girl, Interrupted* (1999); she appears in the movie *Gone in 60 Seconds*.

2001

Jolie appears in the movies *Lara Croft: Tomb Raider* and *Original Sin*; she makes her first trip to refugee camps in Sierra Leone, Cambodia, Tanzania, and Pakistan; she becomes a goodwill ambassador for the UNHCR.

2002

Jolie adopts Maddox; she appears in the movie *Life or Something Like It*.

2003

Jolie and Thornton divorce; she appears in the movies *Lara Croft Tomb Raider: The Cradle of Life* and *Beyond Borders*; her book, *Notes from My Travels*, is published; she receives the Citizen of the World Award; she creates the Maddox Jolie Foundation.

2004

Jolie appears in *Taking Lives*, *Sky Captain and the World of Tomorrow*, *The Fever*, and *Alexander*, and is the voice of a character in *Shark Tale*; she receives the People's Choice Award for *Sky Captain and the World of Tomorrow*; the filming of *Mr. and Mrs. Smith* begins and Jolie and Brad Pitt meet.

2005

Jolie appears in *Mr. and Mrs. Smith*; she adopts Zahara; she receives the United Nations Global Humanitarian Action Award; she becomes a Cambodian citizen.

2006

Jolie appears in the movie *The Good Shepherd*; she gives birth to her first child with Pitt, daughter Shiloh; Pitt adopts Maddox and Zarhara and the childrens' last names are changed to Jolie-Pitt.

2007

Jolie adopts Pax; she appears in the movies *Beowulf* and *A Mighty Heart*; she receives the Freedom Award; Jolie's mother, Marcheline Bertrand, dies.

2008

Jolie gives birth to her second and third children with Pitt, twins Vivienne and Knox; she appears in the movies *Wanted* and *Changeling* and is the voice of character in *Kung Fu Panda*.

2009

Jolie appears in a thirty-second, public-service announcement to commemorate World Refugee Day.

2010

Jolie appears in the movies *Salt* and *The Tourist*.

2011

In the Land of Blood and Honey, a movie that Jolie wrote and directed. is released.

2013

Jolie undergoes a preventive double mastectomy because she tested positive for the gene for breast cancer.

Books

Dennis Abrams. *Angelina Jolie: Actress and Activist.* New York: Chelsea House, 2011. This is a biography about Jolie. It is part of the Women of Achievement series of books. Other titles in the series include *Madonna: Entertainer, Hillary Rodham Clinton: Politician,* and *Amelia Earhart: Aviator.*

Ian Halperin. *Brangelina: The Untold Story of Brad Pitt and Angelina Jolie.* Montreal, Quebec, Canada: Transit, 2009. Filled with personal anecdotes, this book chronicles Jolie's relationship with actor Brad Pitt.

Angelina Jolie. *Notes from My Travels: Visits with Refugees in Africa, Cambodia, Pakistan, and Ecuador.* New York: Pocket Books, 2003. Written by Jolie herself, this book is about her involvement with the United Nations and her travels to refugee camps.

Andrew Morton. *Angelina: An Unauthorized Biography.* New York: St. Martin's, 2010. Written by a well-known biographer, this book provides a detailed look at Jolie's life from childhood onward.

Brent Specher. *Female Force: Angelina Jolie.* Vancouver, WA: Bluewater, 2011. Illustrated by Nuno Nobre, with a cover by Paul Andrew Manton, this is a comic book about Jolie's life. Female Force is a series of comic books about strong women who are shaping today's culture. Other women featured in the series include First Lady Michelle Obama, author J. K. Rowling, and the creator of the Barbie doll, Ruth Handler.

Kathleen Tracy. *Angelina Jolie: A Biography.* Santa Barbara, CA: Greenwood, 2008. This is a biography about Jolie, which includes discussion of her roles as award-winning actress, Hollywood celebrity, philanthropist, and mother.

Internet Sources

Christopher Bagley. "Brad and Angelina: Domestic Bliss." *W Magazine*, July 2005. www.wmagazine.com/celebrities/archive/brad_pitt_angelina_jolie#slide=1.

Richard Cohen. "Angelina Jolie's Movie, Reminding Us This Is No Time to Turn Inward." *Washington Post*, December 12, 2011. www.washingtonpost.com/opinions/angelina-jolies-movie-reminding-us-this-is-no-time-to-turn-inward/2011/12/12/gIQAi0nZqO_story.html.

Sara Davidson, "Angelina Jolie Interview: Mama!" *Reader's Digest*, June 2007. www.rd.com/family/angelina-jolie-on-being-a-mother-of-4/3.

Tom Junod. "Angelina Jolie Dies for Our Sins." *Esquire*, July 20, 2010. www.esquire.com/women/women-we-love/angelina-jolie-interview-pics-0707.

Raina Kelley. "The Secret World of Angelina Jolie." Daily Beast, July 12, 2010. www.thedailybeast.com/newsweek/2010/07/13/the-secret-world-of-angelina-jolie.item-1.html.

Gayle Tzemach Lemmon. "Angelina Jolie's Film Bears Witness to Rape in War." CNN, January 4, 2012. www.cnn.com/2012/01/04/opinion/lemmon-jolie-movie-women-war/index.html.

Cindy Pearlman. "Angelina Jolie on Life with Brad Pitt and Their Brood." *Chicago Sun Times*, December 29, 2011. www.suntimes.com/entertainment/pearlman/9690884-421/angelina-jolie-on-life-with-brad-pitt-and-their-brood.html.

Philip Sherwell. "Angelina Jolie Inflames New Ethnic Emotions in Bosnia with Her Debut as Film Director." *Daily Telegraph* (London), December 17, 2011. www.telegraph.co.uk/culture/film/film-news/8963636/Angelina-Jolie-inflames-new-ethnic-emotions-in-Bosnia-with-her-debut-as-film-director.html.

Robert Siegel. "Angelina Jolie Discusses Her New Movie." NPR, December 23, 2011. www.npr.org/2011/12/23/144195828/angelina-jolie-discusses-her-new-movie.

Periodicals

Brooks Barnes. "Angelina Jolie's Carefully Orchestrated Image." *New York Times*, November 20, 2008.

Rich Cohen. "Angelina: Under Fire." *Vanity Fair*, October 2011.

Rich Cohen. "A Woman in Full." *Vanity Fair*, July 2008.

Angelina Jolie. "Staying to Help in Iraq." *Washington Post*, February 28, 2008.

Angelina Jolie. "My Medical Choice." *The New York Times*, May 14, 2013. http://www.nytimes.com/2013/05/14/opinion/my-medical-choice.html?_r=0

Nicholas Kristof. "Angelina, George, Ben and Mia." *New York Times*, December 31, 2011.

Dotson Rader. "'Salt' Star Angelina Jolie Dishes on Rebellious Past, Run-ins with the Paparazzi and Love for Brad Pitt." *Parade*, July 11, 2010.

Larry Rohter. "Behind the Camera, but Still the Star." *New York Times*, December 6, 2011.

Naomi Wolf. "The Power of Angelina." *Harper's Bazaar*, June 8, 2009.

Websites

Bio.com (www.bio.com). This is the website for the Biography Channel, a cable television channel on the A&E Television Network. It offers biographies about famous people, including Angelina Jolie.

IMDb (www.imdb.com). This is the Internet Movie Database website. It offers information about movies, television shows, and people in the entertainment industry. It includes a biography of Angelina Jolie and a list of her movies.

In the Land of Blood and Honey (www.inthelandofbloodandhoney .com). This is the official site for *In the Land of Blood and Honey*, a movie written and directed by Angelina Jolie. The site includes some information about Jolie's career and humanitarian work in the "Filmmakers" section.

Maddox Jolie-Pitt Foundation (www.mjpasia.org). This is the official website of the Maddox Jolie-Pitt Foundation, a nonprofit organization founded by Angelina Jolie in 2003 to help people in poverty, to protect natural resources, and to protect wildlife around the world. The site offers information on the foundation's efforts and its many projects.

UNHRC: The UN Refugee Agency (www.unhcr.org). This is the official website of the United Nations High Commissioner for Refugees. It offers information about what the agency does, who it helps, and the places where it operates. It also offers information on the work of its goodwill ambassador, Angelina Jolie.

Picture Credits

Cover: © Neil Hall/Reuters/Landov
© Alastair Grant/AFP/Getty Images, 62
© Alex Bailey/Lawrence Gordon/Mutual Film/Paramount/The Kobal Collection/Art Resource, NY, 41
© Andreas Rentz/AFP/Getty Images, 75
© Andrew Schwartz/Universal/The Kobal Collection/Art Resource, NY, 52
© AP Images/Starpix, Dave Allocca, 74
© AP Images/LA(Phot) Iggy Roberts, MOD, 9
© AP Images/Boris Heger, 61
© AP Images/Shawn Baldwin, 66
© Bob Scott/Fotos International/Getty Images, 17
© Carmen Valdes/WireImage/Getty Images, 43
© Gerard Julien/AFP/Getty Images, 73
© Gregg DeGuire/WireImage/Getty Images, 39
© Hal Garb/AFP/Getty Images, 34
© Harry Langdon/Getty Images, 23
© Jane O'Neal/Rysher Entertainment/The Kobal Collection/Art Resource, NY, 27

© Jason Merritt/FilmMagic/Getty Images, 54
© Jason Merritt/Getty Images, 51
© Jim McHugh/TNT/The Kobal Collection/Art Resource, NY, 31
© Jim Smeal/WireImage/Getty Images, 19
© Mark Cuthbert/UK Press via Getty Images, 30
© Natalie Behring-Chisholm/Getty Images, 58
© Neil Mockford/FilmMagic/Getty Images, 68
© Nicholas Kamm/AFP/Getty Images, 70
© Ron Galella/WireImage/Getty Images, 12, 14
© Shkree Sukplang/AFP/Getty Images, 57
© Stephen Vaughan/20th Century Fox/The Kobal Collection/Art Resource, NY, 46
© STR/AFP/Getty Images, 49
© Suzanne Tenner/Columbia Tristar/The Kobal Collection/Art Resource, NY, 37
© United Artists/The Kobal Collection/Art Resource, NY, 26

About the Author

Bonnie Szumski has been an editor and author of nonfiction books for over twenty-five years. Jill Karson has been a writer and editor of nonfiction books for young adults for fifteen years.